PRAISE FOR
THE **WINNING** FAMILY

Today's families need hope and direction now more than ever. That's why I'm excited about *The Winning Family*. My friends Rodney and Michelle Gage have put together a simple, 5-step framework that will help you define—or redefine—your vision for your marriage and family relationships. I'm excited to join the movement of helping families live with greater intention.

—**TobyMac**
Grammy Award-Winning Recording Artist

For over three decades, I've coached young people on how to win on and off the field. If there's one thing a team must have in order to win, it's a solid game plan. But even the best plan requires making adjustments. In *The Winning Family*, Rodney and Michelle Gage not only provide a powerful game plan, but they also show you how to make the right adjustments along the way in your most important relationships. This book can be a game-changer for your marriage and family.

—**Coach Lou Holtz**
Legendary Football Coach

If there was ever a time for families to make a shift and reclaim the eroding spiritual and moral values of our culture, it is now. Rodney and Michelle Gage have provided a simple yet powerful framework to help families stay anchored to God and to each other. I highly recommend *The Winning Family*.

—**Josh McDowell**
Best-Selling Author and Speaker

Winning five World Series taught me that championship teams require chemistry and teamwork. The same is true for families. As a husband and father of four, I know how challenging it can be to overcome the curveballs culture throws at us. *The Winning Family* offers a proven plan to help couples and parents experience victory where it matters most—at home.

—Andy Pettitte
5-Time World Series Champion and 3-Time All-Star

If a marriage or family is going to avoid being swept away by today's culture, they must have a plan. *The Winning Family* gives couples and parents a proven framework to keep their relationships focused on what matters most. If you want to avoid drifting apart, this book is a must-read.

—David and Jason Benham
Best-Selling Authors, Entrepreneurs, and Speakers

No family drifts into health and wholeness. In *The Winning Family*, Rodney and Michelle Gage provide a clear, intentional path for parents to create a life-giving home where children can flourish. I've seen the power of these principles firsthand through Compassion's work around the world. In a culture working against the family, this book is a gift to any parent who wants the best for their children.

—Santiago "Jimmy" Mellado
President and CEO, Compassion International

We are so excited about *The Winning Family*! We love how Rodney and Michelle help couples and families clearly define their own vision, mission, and core values. This book serves as a spiritual and moral compass to help families successfully navigate life in today's world.

—John Luke and Mary Kate Robertson
Duck Dynasty Stars

It takes a lot of prayer, wisdom, and intentionality to keep your family from drifting with the culture. That's why I'm so excited about *The Winning Family*. Rodney and Michelle live the principles they teach. This book gives us a much-needed framework and practical tools to help safeguard our most important relationships.

—**Andi Andrew**
Speaker and Author of *She Is Free* **and** *Fake or Follower*

Success is being loved and respected by those who know you best—and no one knows us better than our own families. In *The Winning Family*, Rodney and Michelle identify five critical shifts to help families win. I highly recommend this book to couples and parents seeking to live with greater purpose and intention.

—**Shawn Lovejoy**
Author, President and CEO of Courage to Lead

We know firsthand how demanding careers can distract from the ones we love most. In *The Winning Family*, Rodney and Michelle provide a clear, 5-step plan to help families realign their priorities and protect what matters most. This book will help you reclaim the heart of your home.

—**David and Nicole Crank**
Senior Pastors, Faith Church, St. Louis, MO, and West Palm Beach, FL

A successful marriage and family don't happen by accident—it takes intention, commitment, and a plan. *The Winning Family* gives couples and parents a step-by-step approach to building healthy homes and strong relationships. Whether you're just starting out, raising kids, or navigating blended family life, this book offers the help and hope every family needs.

—**Dr. Jack Graham**
Senior Pastor, Prestonwood Baptist Church, Dallas, TX

I've known Rodney and Michelle for years and have watched their children develop into amazing leaders. The principles and proven framework in *The Winning Family* are exactly what today's parents need to anchor their families against the cultural currents pulling them apart. This book will give you hope, clarity, and direction to help your family reach its full potential.

—**Layne Schranz**
Vice President of Highlands College Leadership Institute
Pikes Peak Hill Climb Champion

Just as a great dish requires quality ingredients and a solid recipe, a strong family requires the right principles and a proven plan. *The Winning Family* is that plan. Rodney and Michelle offer practical steps and timeless wisdom that will help you turn your house into a home the way God intended.

—**John Rivers**
Chef and Owner, 4 Rivers Smokehouse

A winning family takes work, sacrifice, forgiveness, and above all—love. In *The Winning Family*, Rodney and Michelle reveal five essential shifts that can move your family from where you are to where you want to be. If you're ready to grow stronger together, this book is for you.

—**Dr. Dave Martin**
Best-Selling Author, Pastor, and Success Coach

A strong family isn't built by chance—it's built by choice. *The Winning Family* delivers five powerful shifts every couple can make to protect and strengthen their marriage and family relationships. This is a timely and much-needed resource for every home.

—**Pastors Ed and Lisa Young**
Fellowship Church, Grapevine, TX
NYT Best-Selling Authors

Living with intention is easier said than done, but it's the only way families can thrive in today's world. *The Winning Family* provides the practical tools and spiritual direction to help families stay grounded in what matters most. We highly recommend this book!

—Pastors Bil and Jessica Cornelius
Church Unlimited, Corpus Christi, TX

As a coach, I've seen that strong families produce strong leaders—on and off the field. *The Winning Family* is a game-changing playbook that gives parents the confidence, clarity, and practical tools they need to lead their homes with vision and purpose. Rodney and Michelle have written a must-read for anyone who wants to raise champions in life.

—Coach Denny Duron
Legendary Football Coach
Evangel Christian Academy
Inspiration behind the TV series God. Family. Football.

The Alpha and Gen Z generations are being raised by Millennial and Gen X parents. Why does this matter? Because we often ask parents to disciple their kids without realizing many of them were never discipled themselves. That's why *The Winning Family* is such a timely and needed resource. It equips and empowers parents to embrace one of the greatest callings in their lives—to disciple and minister to their own kids for the glory of God.

—Shane Pruitt
National Next Gen Director, North
American Mission Board (NAMB)

Copyright © 2026 by Rodney and Michelle Gage

Published by The Winning Family

All rights reserved. No portion of this book may be reproduced, stored in a retrieval system, or transmitted in any form or by any means—electronic, mechanical, photocopy, recording, scanning, or other—except for brief quotations in critical reviews or articles, without prior written permission of the author.

Unless otherwise marked, all Scripture quotations are NIV and are taken from the Holy Bible, New International Version®, NIV®. Copyright © 1973, 1978, 1984, 2011 by Biblica, Inc.™ Used by permission of Zondervan. All rights reserved worldwide. www.zondervan.com. The "NIV" and "New International Version" are trademarks registered in the United States Patent and Trademark Office by Biblica, Inc.™ | Scripture quotations marked ESV are from The ESV® Bible (The Holy Bible, English Standard Version®), copyright © 2001 by Crossway, a publishing ministry of Good News Publishers. Used by permission. All rights reserved. | Scripture quotations marked KJV are taken from the King James Version of the Bible. Public domain. | Scripture quotations marked MSG are taken from THE MESSAGE, copyright © 1993, 1994, 1995, 1996, 2000, 2001, 2002 by Eugene H. Peterson. Used by permission of NavPress. All rights reserved. Represented by Tyndale House Publishers, Inc. | Scripture quotations marked NASB are taken from the (NASB®) New American Standard Bible®, Copyright © 1960, 1971, 1977, 1995, 2020 by The Lockman Foundation. Used by permission. All rights reserved. www.lockman.org | Scripture quotations marked NKJV are taken from the New King James Version®. Copyright © 1982 by Thomas Nelson. Used by permission. All rights reserved. | Scripture quotations marked NLT are taken from the Holy Bible, New Living Translation, copyright © 1996, 2004, 2015 by Tyndale House Foundation. Used by permission of Tyndale House Publishers, Inc., Carol Stream, Illinois 60188. All rights reserved. | Scripture quotations marked TLB are taken from The Living Bible copyright © 1971 by Tyndale House Foundation. Used by permission of Tyndale House Publishers Inc., Carol Stream, Illinois 60188. All rights reserved. The Living Bible, TLB, and The Living Bible logo are registered trademarks of Tyndale House Publishers. | Scripture quotations marked TPT are from The Passion Translation®. Copyright © 2017, 2018 by Passion & Fire Ministries, Inc. Used by permission. All rights reserved. ThePassionTranslation.com.

For foreign and subsidiary rights, contact the author.

Cover design by Michael J. Williams and Todd Petelle

ISBN: 978-1-964794-85-3   1 2 3 4 5 6 7 8 9 10

Printed in the United States of America

RODNEY & MICHELLE GAGE

THE WINNING FAMILY

5 Essential Shifts for Parents to Avoid
Drifting and Win at Home

Dedication

This book resulted from the incredible legacy of faith that our parents, Freddie and Barbara Gage and Rod and Linda Masteller, have shared with us through their love for God and each other. Our lives and the lives of our three children are the fruit of the seeds they have sown.

CONTENTS

INTRODUCTION	THE CULTURE SHIFT	15
	STEP 1: START WITH THE END IN MIND	
	A SHIFT IN DIRECTION	23
CHAPTER 1	ON YOUR MARK	25
CHAPTER 2	GET SET	39
CHAPTER 3	GO!	55
	STEP 2: HOLD TO CORE VALUES	
	A SHIFT IN FOCUS	67
CHAPTER 4	FAMILY IS A TEAM SPORT	69
CHAPTER 5	RULE BOOKS, PLAYBOOKS, AND THE GOOD BOOK	83
CHAPTER 6	WHAT GETS REWARDED GETS REPEATED	97
	STEP 3: IDENTIFY YOUR GPS	
	A SHIFT IN MOTIVATION	111
CHAPTER 7	ENVISION THE FUTURE	113
CHAPTER 8	DOING WHAT COMES NATURALLY	131
CHAPTER 9	TOUGHEN UP	147
	STEP 4: FIND LIFE-GIVING FRIENDSHIPS	
	A SHIFT IN REINFORCEMENT	159
CHAPTER 10	IRON SHARPENS IRON	161
CHAPTER 11	EVERY FRIENDSHIP NEEDS A LITTLE TLC	177
	STEP 5: TEACH BY EXAMPLE	
	A SHIFT IN PURPOSE	189
CHAPTER 12	WHO'S ON POINT?	191
CHAPTER 13	THE POWER OF UNCONDITIONAL LOVE	205
CHAPTER 14	LEAVING THE NEST	221
Appendix		235

INTRODUCTION

THE CULTURE SHIFT

AND HOW YOU CAN LEAD YOUR FAMILY THROUGH IT

Every family ends up somewhere, but few end up somewhere on purpose.

Right now, we're living in a time unlike any other in history. The world our kids are growing up in looks vastly different from the one we knew as children. The pace of change is staggering. The values that once shaped strong families and communities are being replaced by a culture that often feels confusing, chaotic, and even hostile to the things we hold dear.

Parents everywhere are feeling the pressure. We see the headlines. We hear the statistics. We watch as childhood innocence is stripped away earlier than ever before, thanks to technology that puts the entire world—including all its dangers—right at our children's fingertips. Social media, smartphones, and endless streams of content are shaping how our kids think, act, and believe. And for many parents, it's terrifying.

How do we protect our children from the negative influences of a culture that's drifting further from truth? How do we equip them with the wisdom and character they need to stand firm in a world that's constantly shifting? How do we raise kids who thrive—spiritually, emotionally, and relationally—when we often feel unprepared and overwhelmed ourselves?

If you've ever wrestled with these questions, you're not alone.

For many parents, the struggle is even deeper because they didn't have strong role models growing up. Maybe that's your story. Maybe you didn't grow up in a home where faith, values, and healthy relationships were prioritized. Maybe you're determined to give your kids something better—but you're not exactly sure how.

Here's the good news: You don't have to figure this out on your own. There is a path forward.

DRIFTING IS DANGEROUS

Years ago, we (Rodney and Michelle) went on a trip to Cancún, Mexico, with Michelle's three sisters, their husbands, and Michelle's mom and dad. While there, one of our most memorable activities was snorkeling. The experience began with us riding WaveRunners through the lagoon's mangrove canals and into the ocean. Our tour guide rode out ahead, leading us to an amazing Caribbean coral reef. Just before we jumped off our watercrafts into the water, he reminded us to adhere to the "check in or check out" rule, which encourages snorkelers to come up to the surface, look around, and "check in" about every ten to fifteen minutes. He wanted us to be aware of our location at all times, because the undercurrent could cause us to drift out to sea. All of us jumped in, put our faces down, and were immediately amazed by the incredible beauty of the underwater world. We explored a beautiful coral reef containing all kinds of colorful fish and unusual creatures. We were so engrossed and distracted that we completely forgot our guide's caution to "check in." Fortunately, he saw that we had drifted too far from the safe zone and blew his whistle to get our attention. If he hadn't, we could have easily drifted farther and farther away until we "checked out." That experience was a wake-up call.

Drift is dangerous—not just in the ocean but in life. And right now, families are drifting.

Not because they want to. Not because they don't care. But because today's culture is an undercurrent, constantly pulling them away from what matters most. Parents are busy, overwhelmed, and distracted—and little by little, without realizing it, they're drifting further from the home they once dreamed of building.

The truth is, families don't drift into winning. They drift into losing. Winning requires intention; drifting happens by default.

Families don't drift into victory. They drift into defeat.

So how do you know if you're drifting? You don't need a GPS tracker or a parenting app to tell you. All you have to do is look at the people around you ... and look in the mirror.

Here are some of the most common warning signs that drift has taken hold:

Distractions and Disappointment

Life is busier than ever. Parents are overcommitted, kids are overscheduled, and downtime has become a luxury. Harvard's School of Public Health reports that nearly half of parents say they feel "rushed" most of the time (Harvard, 2023). The result? The busyness and heartaches of life crowd out the simple joys of connection. Families are present under the same roof but absent in spirit.

Regret

Many parents quietly replay their past mistakes like a highlight reel on repeat. Failures, missed opportunities, or wounds from their own upbringing weigh heavily. Instead of fueling growth, regret keeps them stuck in shame. Drift feeds on regret because regret convinces us that winning isn't possible anymore.

Isolation

Here's what's surprising: families today are more "connected" digitally than at any time in history—and yet loneliness has reached epidemic levels. A 2023 US Surgeon General's report revealed that half of Americans regularly feel lonely, with parents naming isolation as one of their top stressors.[1,2,3] Sometimes others push us away. Other times, we retreat into isolation to feel safe. Either way, drift thrives in disconnection.

Frustration

"Hurry sickness" is real. When families are always rushing from one thing to the next, exhaustion turns into irritation, and irritation turns into frustration. Parents feel stuck. Kids feel like life is just one long grind. Everyone's running, but no one feels like they're winning.

Tension

Unresolved conflict, constant stress, and fear about the future create a home environment where everyone's on edge. The American Psychological Association reports that family conflict—often triggered by money stress, schedules, and technology boundaries—is one of the top predictors of adolescent anxiety.[4] Drift doesn't always shout. Sometimes it simmers quietly in the background through tension and worry.

---

[1] Cigna Corporation, *The Loneliness Epidemic Persists: A Post-Pandemic Look at the State of Loneliness among U.S. Adults* (Bloomfield, CT: Cigna, 2021).

[2] Lisa D. Bruce, Jason S. Wu, Steven L. Lustig, Daniel W. Russell, and David A. Nemecek, "Loneliness in the United States: A 2018 National Panel Survey of Demographic, Structural, Cognitive, and Behavioral Characteristics," *American Journal of Health Promotion* 33, no. 8 (2019): 1123–33.

[3] Brittany Shovestul, Jiyoung Han, Laura Germine, and David Dodell-Feder, "Risk Factors for Loneliness: The High Relative Importance of Age versus Other Factors," *PLOS ONE* 15, no. 2 (2020): e0229087.

[4] American Psychiatric Association, "Resource Document on Social Determinants of Mental Health in Children and Youth," American Psychiatric Association, 2019, https://www.psychiatry.org/getattachment/a03e07c5-bba9-4ac7-b434-9183b1e0b730/Resource-Document-Social-Determinants-of-Mental-Health-Youth.pdf.

When these factors show up in our homes, they're evidence that we've lost focus. Our sense of confidence and purpose gets shaken. And soon, the family we dreamed of becomes the family we're just trying to survive.

But here's the good news: drift doesn't have to define your story. It doesn't have to ruin everything good in your life—not anymore, at least. You can change. You can win. And the very fact that you're reading this book proves that you want something better.

THE CULTURE HAS SHIFTED—IT'S TIME TO TAKE THE LEAD

The truth is, it's never been more difficult to raise a family with strong values. The culture around us is changing at a rapid pace, redefining truth, morality, and identity.

What once seemed clear is now clouded by confusion.

What was once protected is now exposed.

What was once honored is now ridiculed.

And the ones caught in the middle of this cultural shift? Our children.

As parents, we have two choices:

1) **We can be reactive**—constantly trying to keep up, putting out fires, and hoping our kids turn out okay.
2) **Or we can be intentional**—leading our families with a clear vision, equipping our kids to stand strong, and creating a home where faith and values are the foundation.

If we don't take the lead, culture will.

If we don't give our kids a solid foundation, the world will shape them instead.

And that's why we're here.

We believe that winning at home is the key to winning in life. If we want our kids to thrive, we must be intentional about shaping their hearts, minds, and character before the world does. That means taking a proactive approach to parenting—not just hoping for the best but having a plan, a strategy, and a roadmap to navigate every phase of the journey.

THE ROADMAP TO INTENTIONAL PARENTING

For over thirty-four years, we've devoted our lives to helping families stop drifting and start living with greater intention. Not because we've done everything perfectly—trust us, we've made our share of mistakes—but because we've seen firsthand what happens when parents take ownership of their role as the primary influence in their children's lives.

We don't know what brought you to this book. Maybe you're just starting your parenting journey, and you want to get it right from the beginning. Maybe you're in the thick of raising kids and feeling overwhelmed by the daily pressures. Or maybe you're watching your teenagers struggle, and you're desperate for a way to reconnect before it's too late.

Wherever you are, you're not alone. And no matter how far you've drifted, it's never too late to make a shift.

THE FIVE SHIFTS EVERY PARENT MUST MAKE

In the pages ahead, we'll walk you through **five essential shifts** that will help you build a strong, connected, and faith-filled family. Every family needs to make a shift in ***direction, focus, motivation, reinforcement, and purpose.*** These are not quick fixes or parenting hacks. They are time-tested principles that will guide you through every season of raising kids—from toddlers to teenagers and beyond.

The five shifts are:

Start with the End in Mind: Get clear on the kind of family you want to build and the legacy you want to leave.

Hold to Core Values: Establish unshakable beliefs that will guide your family through every challenge.

Identify Your GPS (Goals, Passions, and Struggles): Understand what drives each member of your family and navigate the roadblocks that try to derail you.

Find Life-Giving Friendships: Surround yourself with people who will support, encourage, and challenge you in your parenting journey.

Teach by Example: Live out the values you want to see in your children, because the greatest lessons are caught, not just taught.

Whether your family is thriving or struggling, whether you're confident or feeling completely unprepared, **you can lead your family well.** You don't have to be a perfect parent—you just need to be an intentional one.

Are you ready? Let's stop the drift and make the shift.

Before you go any further, make this declaration:

I declare a SHIFT is coming—

A SHIFT in my thinking.

A SHIFT in my purpose.

A SHIFT in my priorities.

A SHIFT in my marriage.

A SHIFT in my family relationships.

A SHIFT in my future.

Let's do this—together.

STEP 1

START WITH THE END IN MIND

A SHIFT IN DIRECTION

CHAPTER 1

ON YOUR MARK

TAKE AN HONEST LOOK AT YOUR PAST AND PRESENT

You cannot change your destination overnight, but you can change your direction overnight.
—Jim Rohn[5]

One of the perks of living in Orlando is the convenience of being able to drive over to the local attractions and theme parks for a day of fun. One day, we decided to go to Disney's Magic Kingdom for the day. Our three kids, Becca, Ashlyn, and Luke, were much younger at the time. For some reason, we chose to go on a day when half of the planet's population was there. After fighting through the crowds for hours, we

---
5 Jim Rohn, "4 Straightforward Steps to Success," *SUCCESS Magazine*, March 31, 2015, updated October 7, 2023, https://www.success.com/rohn-4-straightforward-steps-to-success/.

enjoyed a number of rides, shows, shops, and other amusements. As we got ready for the next adventure, we gathered up our clan . . . but we didn't see Luke. I (Rodney) scanned the immediate area. Nothing. I asked Michelle, "You have Luke, don't you?" She shook her head, and when our eyes met, she instantly realized I didn't know where he was. I asked the girls, "Have you seen Luke?" Neither of them had any idea where he was. Now all of us were in full-blown panic mode!

We searched the area like crazy people, but we couldn't find him anywhere. Of course, in these moments, news reports of missing and kidnapped children flashed in our minds. After a long and frantic but empty search, we asked one of the cast members at Disney World where a missing child might be taken. He pointed us to something like a Human Lost and Found department. When we got there, Luke looked like nothing in the world was wrong. It was a great relief and a joy-filled reunion. I didn't let him get more than a foot away from me the rest of the day.

FAMILY DRIFT

It's easy to lose something you value . . . like a child, a marriage, family relationships, or even a dream you've held in your heart for years. Wise parents acknowledge that even in the best of families, things can go wrong, sometimes much more quickly than they would ever expect. Although research bears out that most people believe that the family is still an important and essential institution, not all the news is good. A 2017 Barna research study states:

> *The family continues to be the institution that most defines us. Family is ranked by American adults as more central to their identity than any other surveyed factor (i.e., being an American, faith, ethnicity, etc.). More than six in 10 (62%) also say that family plays a significant role in their identity ("a lot").*[6]

---

[6] Barna Group, "Forming Family Values in a Digital Age," June 27, 2017, https://www.barna.com/research/forming-family-values-digital-age/.

However, the research also shows a steady decline in each generation. While 76% of the Silent Generation (1925–1945) said that family made up "a lot" of their identity, the Boomers (1946–1964) had dropped to 64%, the Gen-Xers (1965–1976) to 61%, and the Millennials (1977–1995) to 53%.[7] It doesn't take a math whiz to detect a disturbing trend here—and it's ever-growing in today's advanced digital world. More recent research suggests that technology has negatively impacted family bonding time and communication.[8]

As family mentors, we can't think of a better term than drift to describe the growing threat we see among families in our culture today. It describes exactly what happens to most couples in their marriage, and it always affects their kids. Even Christian couples usually start with firm commitments to strong, loving relationships based on a spiritual and moral foundation. But at some point, without even realizing it, parents begin to focus more and more on their work schedules and financial demands, and their kids become more involved in academic requirements and extracurricular activities. Before they know it, the once close-knit family finds itself at various stages of emotional distance, and some need only a little shift to get back on track, but others need an extreme home makeover!

We believe most families start out with the best of intentions, but the snorkeling "check in" rule applies here too. The excitement of having children and enjoying all the developmental stages of their young lives, coupled with the many time-consuming responsibilities of parenthood, can cause parents to move into survival mode. Over time, imperceptibly, the increasing demands of work, financial pressure, and endless busyness create a dangerous drift away from the family connections that once seemed unbreakable. When family members fail to regularly raise their heads to "check in" and see where they are spiritually, morally, and

---

7 "Forming Family Values in a Digital Age."

8 Ashwini Tadpatrikar et al., "Influence of technology usage on family communication patterns and functioning: A systematic review," Asian *Journal of Psychiatry* 58 (2021), https://doi.org/10.1016/j.ajp.2021.102595.

relationally, they eventually drift further away from God and His plans and purposes for their family. They "check out" and begin to drown in the sea of problems: family conflict, wayward kids, marriage trouble, and quite often, divorce.

In our world, this is the point when we get the phone call. A marriage or a child is drowning, and families are crying out for help. They've found themselves drifting away from the security and satisfaction they once shared in the home. Now, they wonder if being rescued is even possible. Sadly, this condition has become the norm, not the exception.

> *Drift is automatic. Winning is intentional.*
> —Rodney and Michelle Gage

In all our years of working with families, here's what we know to be true: *Your direction, not your intention, will lead you to your destination.* In other words, no matter how sincerely you intend to raise spiritually and morally strong kids, it doesn't just happen. The truth is that the direction your marriage and family are moving right now along the path you have set with your values, commitments, and priorities will ultimately determine your destination.

In our roles, we see many young parents highly involved in their children's lives when they start school. The parents volunteer, show up for parent/teacher meetings, and donate money for worthy causes to help the school and community. In addition, they sign their children up for all kinds of extracurricular activities: Little League sports, Boy Scouts and Girl Scouts, dance, cheerleading, music lessons, and the list goes on and on. Clearly, the parents' intentions are heartfelt. They want the very best for their children.

As the kids grow up, their activities demand even more time and money. In addition, academic priorities become a consuming focus. Parents discover that most of the better public and private universities look for a high-achieving record of accomplishments before a child will even be considered for acceptance. Parents feel a tremendous amount of tension to figure out how to balance the demands of school, all the extracurricular activities, work schedules, and basic household responsibilities.

You already know this, of course—or if your kids are still very young, you'll find out soon enough. The point is that we need more than good intentions to raise strong families. Intentions won't prevent drift. We need to assess and address the direction we're moving. Are we allowing cultural drift to gradually take us further away from where we really want to be? Or are we making a persistent effort to stop the drift, recalculate, and do whatever it takes to move back in a direction that will take us to a place where we and our kids thrive?

LOOK UP AND LOOK AROUND

An old saying tells us, "If you keep doing the same thing you've always done, you'll keep getting the same results you've always gotten." Once you realize that drift has become a problem in your family, and especially if you detect that you are continuing to drift with no control over the situation, it's time for you to act—to do something different.

The vast majority of people don't intend to drift away from what's most important to them. Consequently, even fewer people don't have an idea of what a loving, strong family can look like. For them, drift is inevitable. They may have grown up in broken homes, with absent parents, single parents, unloving foster care homes, or without any understanding of what a true, solid family could look like. From our interactions with thousands of people, we've identified six primary reasons families drift no matter your familial background or good intentions. These can be present to a minor or major degree, and families may experience one or more of them at the same time.

1) They don't have a clear vision of what family life can be.

   All they've seen in their parents, extended family, and other families is people who barely tolerate each other, whose anger either leads to explosions or implosions, and whose goal is only to survive another day without too much trauma or drama.

2) They don't have a set of guiding values that shape their decisions and interactions.

   They've absorbed their values—that is, what's most important to them—from their parents and from the culture, and they've never even considered outlining how they can relate to each other.

3) They confuse their priorities with their commitments.

   They've made commitments of time and energy to various activities before they established a priority list that would help them include some activities and eliminate others.

4) They don't do enough to protect their family from powerful, though often attractive, negative influences.

   The culture's supreme values of success, pleasure, and approval seem perfectly reasonable because they're so pervasive. But when we treasure those things above God and His purposes, we become vulnerable to temptation and deception. And with technology, our kids are exposed to far more negative influences than we could have ever imagined when we were in school.

5) They focus on each other's faults instead of their strengths.

   Hurt people hurt people. When people feel empty and wounded, they become as prickly as porcupines!

6) Their deepest needs for security and love aren't met, so they operate out of a deficiency instead of an overflow of gratitude.

We need to look deeper, to uncover the truth about our deepest wounds and highest desires, and make sure we experience God's love, forgiveness, and strength. The deepest issues in our lives aren't the words we use when we talk to each other, but the source of those words. Jesus said, "Out of the abundance of the heart the mouth speaks" (Matthew 12:34, ESV). Just trying to corral our words may work for a few minutes but not for long.

Do any of these sound familiar?

Let's return to the lesson we learned on the day of snorkeling: If you were in the ocean and realized that drift had become a serious threat, you'd take action and change direction. Ironically, most of us are probably better prepared to handle a crisis in the ocean than the problem of drift in our own homes. Ocean swimmers have a plan; they're taught that in the event of a rip tide carrying them out to sea, they shouldn't panic. They shouldn't attempt a mad swim directly back to shore against the strong current. Instead, they're instructed to swim parallel to the shore until they get out of the potentially deadly current and then swim diagonally toward the shore to safety. Likewise we must have a plan for our families.

THINK *WHO* BEFORE *DO*

We believe there are two crucial questions all of us need to ask ourselves:

1) Who do I want to be as a husband or wife and as a parent?

Far too often, husbands and wives lose their sense of vision, purpose, and meaning, so the best they can imagine is to struggle through another day with as little hassle as possible. The currents of the culture sweep them downstream. They're drifting, but they don't even notice. They become wrapped up in secondary things and miss the most important things in their own lives and their families. Soon, their passion for life has been replaced with too many regrets. It may help to expand this question into specifics. Together, you should answer: Who do we want to be as a couple? Who do we want to be as a family? And individually answer: Who do I want to be as a mom or a dad? It's important to start to regain that vision by asking these questions . . . and spending plenty of time answering them. Once we understand who we want to be, we can then focus on what we need to do.

2) **Is there a "desire gap" between how things are now and what I feel "ought" to be?**

The "desire gap" is the distance between where you are right now and who you want to be. After you've answered the first question, this one focuses on the challenge of change. Your gap may be large or small, but whatever the size, we all need tangible steps and fuel for our passions to motivate us to close the desire gap in our lives. The deepest issues in our lives aren't the words we use when we talk to each other, but the source of those words. Jesus said, "Out of the abundance of the heart [the] mouth speaks" (Luke 6:45 NKJV). Change is the bridge between who you are and who you want to become. Based upon whom you desire to be, you will need to make changes and stop certain behaviors. Shifting takes courage

> *When we get our* who *right, we get our* what *right!*
> —Rodney and Michelle Gage

We'll be honest with you. The sooner you notice the effects that drifting can have on your family, the easier it will be to make the adjustments and get back on course. But we suspect that many people have picked up this book because they're in various stages of going under. The longer we wait to acknowledge we're drifting, the more it can pull us down spiritually, morally, emotionally, relationally, and financially. If that's your case, let us assure you: It's never too late to make a shift that will restore your family to peaceful waters and smooth sailing, no matter what stage of the parenting journey you're on.

IT'S NEVER TOO LATE

We've had the privilege of seeing God work in the lives of individuals, couples, and families to bring dramatic and lasting change. Here are just a few:

- Suzanne is a single mother who felt traumatized by her husband's infidelity and unwillingness to make any changes in his priorities. A year after the divorce, she could barely make it through work each day, and she had very little energy left for her two children, eight and twelve years old. She joined a group that helped her experience God's love, grieve her deep hurts, and find God's purpose for her as a daughter of the King and as a mother. Today, she is one of the most joyful people we know.
- Jarod and Alicia scheduled two appointments, one with a counselor and the other with an attorney. If the first one didn't go well, they were going to the attorney to get a divorce. Both of them had good jobs, but they had spent far beyond their income. The strain of trying to pay interest on their debt each month caused them to blame each other, and their kids were often the object of their anger if they did anything remotely wrong. The counselor gave them hope that their matrix of problems—debt, marital stress, and children out of control—could be resolved in a process of healing, a commitment to speak to each other with grace, and finding a financial counselor who could help them with their debt. Hope had a miraculous effect. They soon were talking to each other with respect, they didn't bark at their children, and they began to see light at the end of the financial tunnel.
- Jenny had been physically and emotionally abused by her father, so she had great difficulty trusting men, including her husband, Robert. She was emotionally fragile, so anything less than complete and perfect affection offended her and caused her to withdraw. Poor Robert never saw this coming. Before they married, he knew Jenny had some problems with her father, but when she finally told him the truth, her behavior made a lot more sense. Together, they found a way forward, discovering deeper love and security than either of them had ever known before.

- Carlos and Maria had enjoyed the good life before they had kids. They traveled, Carlos fished, and Maria enjoyed her work and lunches with friends. They assumed that having kids would fit nicely into their priorities. It didn't. The demands of parenthood challenged their priorities and made them irritable with each other and with their little children. When they finally realized their resentment was ruining their family, they decided to get help. They met with an older couple who had weathered many storms in their marriage, and the older couple helped them reframe their expectations. Finally, Carlos and Maria had something bigger and better to live for than fun.

We could describe countless other couples and families that are struggling with everything from the normal strains of life to the ravages of addiction, depression, debt, abuse, and isolation. We talk to men and women who have tried to find solace in the arms of someone else. The pursuit was thrilling for a while, but it devastated their marriage and their kids. We know families who smile and look put together on the outside but behind closed doors suffer from outbursts of rage and shattered hearts. Pornography is so common that it has become an epidemic, even in the Christian community. Some say that it's harmless, but we know it's anything but. It reshapes the viewers' perspective of sexuality and causes them to be dissatisfied with anything but gorgeous and seductive people—people unlike their spouse or anyone they might date. We've seen parents push their kids to excel in academics and sports, so they could get into the best schools and win scholarships. If they get in, they enter a world of even more pressure, and if they don't, they're crushed by a failure they assume will ruin their lives.

If there's one thing we (Rodney and Michelle) are known for, beyond the love we have for each other and our three children, it's our passion to see families challenge the norm by living with greater intention. Through the years, I (Rodney) have had the opportunity to speak to millions of teenagers through school assemblies. Michelle and I have worked with hundreds of couples and families whose lives and relationships have tragically fallen apart. Why are we telling you this? Because raising spiritually, emotionally, and morally strong and secure children and having a healthy, thriving marriage doesn't just happen. As a matter of fact, I believe it's more difficult for a marriage and family to thrive in today's culture—spiritually, morally, and relationally—than ever before.

That's why we're convinced families suffering from drift or want to avoid it all together need more than just prayer; they need a plan. Knowing what to do can help you close the distance between where you are now and where you want to be as a family. We've come to this conclusion based on the trials and errors, as well as successes, our family has experienced. We have received lots of help along the way from other parents who have shared their wisdom and advice with us, which we'll pass along. The five-step plan we're using as a framework for this book has been field-tested with our own family and families in our church, along with families across the country.

The good news is that we don't have to keep perpetuating the same hurts, habits, and hang-ups from our own family experiences. We don't have to pass them on to our children. With God's help, we can make the shift.

Yesterday ended last night. Tomorrow's pages are blank. Today, you can begin to make an improvement in your marriage and family. We're praying for you that God will bring healing to your past and reconciliation and restoration to your relationships today. We believe God can use you and your family in ways you never thought possible. We have no doubt that He can turn your pain into a platform to tell a new story about you and your family.

> *That's why we're convinced families suffering from drift*
> *need more than just prayer; they need a plan.*
> —Rodney and Michelle Gage

THE LAW OF DIMINISHING INTENT

The late Jim Rohn was a business consultant, author, and speaker who had valuable insights that translated into every area of life. One of his most important discoveries was "The Law of Diminishing Intent," which states: "The longer you wait to do something you should do now, the greater the odds that you will never actually do it."[9] You instinctively know it's true. When you know the right thing to do, the longer you wait to do it, the more excuses, new roadblocks, and apathy seem to appear. Initial enthusiasm and conviction can soon lapse into "It was a good idea," and then become "Why was I even thinking about that?"

Every chapter in this book has action points, specific things you and your family can do to identify your purpose and pursue it with all your heart. But know this: You'll want to wait, you'll come up with reasons why they won't matter, and you'll assume your spouse or kids will be so resistant that every attempt is just a waste of time. Don't believe it! *Lean into action.* Sure, you'll make some mistakes, but you'll learn from them. If you sit on the bench, you'll never score any points. It's safer to sit out, but it leads to a life of discontent and emptiness. I hope you'll realize you can take steps forward as you read every page. Take them. Don't wait, or your intent and your enthusiasm will gradually waste away. And then, the only thing that will change is an increase in discouragement.

Some of us are afraid of our desires because they've been shattered so often before, but don't be afraid of your desire for a loving, healthy family. This longing is the first step in leaving a legacy for generations to come. Our prayer is that this book will prompt you to experience a shift unlike anything you have ever known. As you continue reading, keep in mind God's challenge and God's promise from Isaiah, a prophet who lived about 2,500 years ago:

---

9   Sara Gilbert, "How The Law Of Diminishing Intent Nearly Killed My Business," *Forbes Coaches Council*, February 10, 2017, https://www.forbes.com/sites/forbescoachescouncil/2017/02/10/how-the-law-of-diminishing-intent-nearly-killed-my-business/.

Forget about what's happened; don't keep going over old history. Be alert, be present. I'm about to do something brand-new. It's bursting out! Don't you see it? There it is! I'm making a road through the desert, rivers in the badlands. —Isaiah 43:18-19 (MSG)

As Jesus began His ministry, He also read from the book of Isaiah and proclaimed: "This is God's time to shine!" (Luke 4:16-21, MSG). Not next year. Not five or ten years from now. We believe *this* is the year God will help you shift your most important relationships in a new direction.

By the way, we're not assuming you know your way around the Bible. We believe it is the source of wisdom and encouragement that God uses to transform individuals and families. We're using a number of different translations to make the points as clear as possible. We have built our lives, values, and beliefs on the book Jesus fulfilled and validated as God's Word to us, and we're sure God will use it in your life, too. Let's be clear: Most of what you'll read in this book is countercultural. It's different from the assumptions the vast majority of people make each day. God's Word is encouraging because it tells us about God's amazing grace, forgiveness, and love, but it also challenges us to see things from God's point of view and take action based on His purpose and values. God created the family. It's His idea. In the Bible, He has given us a blueprint to follow as we build strong families that can resist the constant push of the culture's current. So, as you read passages from the Bible in these pages, open your heart to hear from God Himself. He's speaking to you through His Word.

At the end of each chapter, you'll find some questions designed to stimulate personal reflection and interaction with your spouse and perhaps a small group of couples who recognize the need to make a shift. The goal isn't to get through them as quickly as possible, but to let them prompt analysis (in the "Think About It" sections) and a commitment to take bold steps forward (when you're prompted to "Do It").

THINK ABOUT IT:
1) If you could only use five words to describe your childhood family, what would they be?
2) Did growing up in your family create any unhealthy habits or behaviors that you have since overcome? Are you aware of any lingering habits that still need to be addressed and corrected?
3) What are some examples of drift you've witnessed in today's culture (in politics, education, churches, etc.)?
4) What are the forces and temptations that cause drift in families? Which of these has been a problem for your family?
5) How frequently do you "check in" to see if you may have drifted further than you realized from God's plan and purpose for your life? When was the last time you checked in for an honest analysis?
6) If you're reading this book, you have good intentions. Would you also say you have a destination in mind? If so, what is it? (And if not, the next chapter will help you think it through.)

DO IT:
Answer and discuss these questions as a family:
1) Who do I want to be as a husband or wife and as a parent?
2) What does the "desire gap" look like for me and my family?

CHAPTER 2

GET SET

CREATE A FAMILY VISION AND MISSION

It's just as difficult to reach a destination you don't have as it is to come back from a place you've never been.
—Zig Ziglar[10]

In our book *ReThink Life*[11], I (Rodney) share an embarrassing moment that took place several years ago at my son's class field trip to Jungle Adventures, one of Florida's original theme parks. At the time, Luke was bound to a wheelchair, so his teacher permitted us to drive separately.

---

10 Zig Ziglar, *See You at the Top* (New Orleans, LA: Pelican Publishing, 2000).
11 Rodney Gage and Michelle Gage, *ReThink Life: How to Be Different from the Norm* (Bloomington, IN: WestBowPress, 2015).

She told us to follow the yellow school buses to the park. I was sure the day would create a lot of fun memories for Luke and me.

I didn't bother to get directions because there was no way to lose a big, yellow bus, but Luke's teacher gave me her cellphone number just in case we got separated. As we approached a major intersection, I decided to go around the bus in front of us, so Luke could wave to his friends. When I pulled back into the lane, we were in front of the bus we'd been following. Several other yellow school buses were lined up in front of us at a stoplight. When the light turned green, the buses in front of us turned right and drove up the onramp of the interstate. I followed them, even though it seemed a bit odd that the buses behind us went straight instead of turning right. I really didn't give it too much thought because I was confident I was doing the right thing by following the buses in front of me.

But soon, doubts began to surface. What if we were supposed to have followed the other buses? This *was* the way to Jungle Adventures, wasn't it? Unwavering in my resolve to keep following the yellow buses, about thirty minutes later, we all finally pulled into a parking lot with a huge alligator head beside a sign that read "Gatorland." With a perplexed look on his face, Luke exclaimed, "Wait a minute, Dad! This is not where our class is going! We're supposed to be at Jungle Adventures."

About that time, my cellphone rang. Luke's teacher asked, "Did you get lost?"

I stammered, "We're, uh, at Gatorland!" Luke and I raced across town to join his class. I'd done exactly what I thought was right, but it was very wrong. I followed the buses, but I followed the wrong buses.

As we established in the previous chapter, it doesn't matter how sincere your intentions may be; if you're headed in the wrong direction with your marriage and family relationships, you'll almost certainly end up at a place you never intended to be.

If we don't have a specific destination in mind—as an individual, family, business, nonprofit, church, or whatever—we're always at risk of drift.

So now let us ask you: Do you know where you want to go as a family? Is your family going somewhere on purpose? Do you have a specific destination—distinct goals—in mind for your family relationships? Or are you perhaps following the wrong bus?

The key to experiencing a relationally and spiritually strong family is to start with the end in mind. Starting does require asking some tough, reflective questions. Where do you see your marriage in the future? What kind of marriage do you want to have? How will you stay devoted and faithful to each other through the challenging seasons of raising children and growing in your career? How will you stay true and committed to each other when you face hardships and trials? What do you want for your children's futures? What kind of people do you want them to become as they enter their teens and adulthood? How will they learn to avoid temptations? How will they learn to make wise choices? That's why it's so important to start with the end in mind. We've already made the point, but we want to emphasize it again: Every family *ends up somewhere*, but few *end up somewhere on purpose*.

THE IMPORTANCE OF MISSION AND VISION

We usually think of the words *mission* and *vision* in a business context, but every good endeavor needs crystal clear direction. Scripture gives us fair warning: "Where there is no vision, the people perish" (Proverbs 29:18, KJV). A more recent interpretation puts it this way: "If people can't see what God is doing, they stumble all over themselves" (Proverbs 29:18, MSG). In other words, when people lose their "why," they lose their way.

It has always amazed us how major companies and nonprofits invest time and money in writing both a mission statement (to explain why the organization exists) and a vision statement (to define where they want to go). Yet, when it comes to the most important institution God created—the family—we seem to just cross our fingers and hope for the best. No wonder so many married couples, kids, and families "stumble all over themselves."

> *Ask yourself if what you are doing today is getting you closer to where you want to be tomorrow.*
> —Dr. Dave Martin[12]

Having a clearly stated mission and vision for your life, marriage, and family will provide four key benefits:

1) **Passion:** Our purpose is fueled by our passion. When we have a clear mission and vision for our marriage and family, we feel energized and empowered to make it happen. The opposite of love isn't hate. It's *apathy*. When we lose our passion for God and the people He has given us to love and protect, we become complacent. We begin to take each other for granted, and we find ourselves merely coexisting, which leads to drifting. Knowing your "why" and keeping it in front of you will fuel your passion to live intentionally every day.

2) **Motivation:** Life is hard. Having a healthy and thriving marriage and a close-knit family is difficult to achieve in today's culture. However, when we have a clear mission and vision for what *should* be and *could* be for our families, we're motivated to keep fighting for what matters most. It's easy to feel overwhelmed and discouraged. A clear mission and vision will give us the motivation we need to push through the difficulties in life.

3) **Direction:** When you start with the end in mind, you always have a "North Star" to guide you. It will keep you from following the wrong bus. Of course, we all get off track at times. We may even get completely turned around. But a clear vision statement works like

---

12   Dr. Dave Martin, "Miracle Mindset | Dr. Dave Martin | Twin Rivers Church," Filmed at Twin Rivers Church, 34:02, *YouTube*, https://www.youtube.com/watch?v=ClDIaE_pDYw.

a compass to help us continually adjust our course and start moving again in the right direction.

4) **Purpose:** Life is too short to live only for ourselves and secondary things (at best). We were made for more. We were made to make a difference. If your family has a pulse, it has a purpose. Your family was not meant to merely survive; it was meant to thrive! Jesus said, "The thief comes only to steal and kill and destroy; I have come that they may have life, and have it to the full" (John 10:10, NIV).

> *Planning is bringing the future into the present so you can do something about it now.*
> —Alan Lakein[13]

ANYONE AND EVERYONE

It's never too early to get serious about putting together a family mission and vision . . . and it's never too late! Couples with young children are certainly at a prime time to initiate a discussion of why the family exists and what future goals they want to work toward. As the children grow, they will always have those guidelines to keep them grounded and growing. However, *anyone* can benefit from creating a vision and mission statement:

- *Singles* can get an early start on considering future family goals. What could be more important than determining a mission and vision for their life? Identifying their desired destination is the best way to find like-minded and spiritually compatible prospects when they begin to search for a suitable mate. And if they remain single, they need a clear and compelling sense of purpose to make life exciting and fulfilling.

---

[13] Bryan Paul Buckley citing Alan Lakein, "How Planning Can Bring the Future Into the Present," *Elite Road Warrior*, February 15, 2021, https://eliteroadwarrior.com/how-planning-can-bring-the-future-into-the-present/.

- *Couples without kids* can benefit from producing a mission and vision statement even before children are in the picture. It's good to have a plan in place before kids start arriving and "extra" time suddenly disappears. Quite often, a pregnancy prompts couples to dream about what their family can become. Those months are a great time to think, plan, imagine, and pray about the future.
- Even *empty nesters and grandparents* should consider: "What kind of legacy do I want to leave my family?" These people have time on their hands again, so they can consider how they can influence those they care most about.

My (Michelle's) dad has four daughters and eleven grandkids, and he stayed extremely active and busy before he suddenly passed away in 2020 as a result of COVID. Every time we got together as a family, he would be very intentional in reminding us that he prayed for us by name every day. He specifically would pray three things over us: God's *presence*, God's *protection*, and God's *provision* for our lives. Then he would ask the kids to repeat back what he had just said. It was his goal to leave us with this reminder and with a better understanding of why we existed as a family. His spiritual influence on our lives was his greatest legacy. To quote Andy Stanley: "Your greatest contribution to the kingdom of God may not be something you do, but someone you raise."[14]

The psalmist tells us: "Take delight in the Lord, and he will give you your heart's desires. Commit everything you do to the Lord. Trust him, and he will help you" (Psalm 37:4-5, NLT). He attaches no age limitations. It's never too soon to start considering your heart's desires—as individuals or as a family. It's never too late to revisit what is most important to you. If you've crafted a mission statement and a vision statement for an organization, transfer the same process to help write one for your family. And if you've never created these statements, let us help you get started.

---

14 Andy Stanley, Twitter post, April 17, 2013, 10:38 pm, https://twitter.com/andystanley/status/324713440541290498.

> *You become what you behold.*
> —Rodney and Michelle Gage

WRITING YOUR MISSION AND VISION STATEMENT

Your mission/purpose statement and vision statement should work hand in hand. Each addresses a specific question, and they complement one another.

As you see from this diagram, there are actually four components to this planning process: mission, values, vision, and strategy. In our experience, we've found it helpful at first to narrow the focus to two: mission and vision. Values shape our mission, and strategy/plan fleshes out the vision, but we'll focus primarily on the main two because if we get those right, the other two follow fairly easily.

Your family mission/purpose statement should answer the question, "Why do I (or we) exist?" As you live and grow together, you need to determine your goals for your life. Another way to ask this is, "What impact will we have on people now, and what legacy will we leave for those who come after us?" You'll probably come up with more than one answer or have multiple sentences. That's great, but make sure it's not too cumbersome and complicated. The mission statement needs to fit easily on the back of a business card. If it's too long or too complex, keep working on it until it's easy to remember. If it's not memorable, it's not going to be captured in your heart.

A subset of the mission is a set of clear values. Here you should answer the question, "What do we care about?" Your answer may be a series of words or phrases that reflect your purpose, and these words could be incorporated into the mission statement.

Since this statement is a family document, it's important that everyone weighs in about what's important to them. Younger children will have more simplistic goals, and teenagers are likely be more ambitious, but their responses are equally important. Since you want the mission statement to apply to everyone in the family, each member should be included in its creation.

> *In planning anything, the best place to begin is at the end. What outcome do you want?*
> —Michael Hyatt and Daniel Harkavy[15]

The process is as important—and maybe *more* important—than the product itself. Don't be in too much of a hurry to get something down on paper. It's possible to sit down and write out a mission/purpose statement in a few minutes, but it's much better to have a series of family discussions and let your family mission naturally evolve from your questions and interactions. If you don't put a lot of thought into writing it, family members probably won't value it or embrace it as a guide.

To give you an example, here is our family's mission/purpose statement, but feel free to create your own format or design:

---

15 Michael Hyatt and Daniel Harkavy, *Living Forward: A Proven Plan to Stop Drifting and Get the Life You Want* (Grand Rapids, MI: Baker Books, 2016).

THE GAGE FAMILY MISSION STATEMENT

The Gage family exists to *Love, Lead, Learn, Laugh, and Live:*
Love God and others the way God loves us;
Lead by example in order to use our influence
to make a difference in people's lives;
Learn from our successes and mistakes: Failure is never final.
Laugh and have fun. Don't take ourselves so
seriously. Make others smile, and
Live each day to its fullest; live with no regrets.

After your *mission/purpose* statement defines "Why do we exist?" the family *vision* statement should answer the question, "Where are we going?" The mission statement is aspirational; the vision statement should be a more practical, hands-on application of the mission and purpose as a family.

Again, if possible, all family members should have input into the creation of the vision statement. Their contribution helps them understand the power of the vision to give motivation and direction. The more personal it is, the more practical and important it will be. Here is our family's vision statement:

THE GAGE FAMILY VISION STATEMENT

Our Vision is to be a family that lives differently from the norm by standing up and standing out for Jesus so that we will win others to Christ and continue our family's legacy for generations to come.

A clear vision can provide confidence to stand firm on your beliefs, values, and decisions, especially when they're different from the norm of our mainstream culture. Your vision will almost certainly attract critics and naysayers at times. I call those people *vision vandals*. But your clear vision, fueled with a passion for what should be, will also give you the determination to see that vision become a reality.

In her book, *Switch on Your Brain,* Dr. Caroline Leaf confirms from a brain science perspective that when you visualize your future, it activates a part of your brain called the reticular activating system (RAS). This acts like your brain's internal spotlight. In other words, once you know what you want and who you're striving to become, your brain begins filtering out distractions and focusing on that goal.[16]

When our daughter Becca became a freshman in high school, she tried out for the cheerleading team, and she made it. I (Michelle) was really proud of her but found out really fast that the other moms took cheerleading a whole lot more seriously than we did. They insisted on having control of every aspect of the girls' lives, and of course, they didn't always agree with each other. I guess that is why some people referred to the moms as "drama mamas." Being on the team is very competitive, and for the girls who make it, it can be very exclusive. About the time Becca was beginning her cheerleading practices, she also found a passion to help lead singing in our church's youth group. The conflict of time was an issue, but so was the conflict of values. After a while, one passion grew and the other ebbed away. Becca decided to drop off the cheerleading team after her freshman year and focus her time and energy on music. Immediately, the other girls treated her like she had leprosy. Following her heart caused Becca to pay a price in her relationships, but she wasn't the only one. Some of the parents of girls on the team treated us with the same contempt. They felt betrayed that our daughter had a mind of her own and chose to do something else with her life. This situation told us

---

16   Dr. Caroline Leaf, *Switch on Your Brain: The Key to Peak Happiness, Thinking, and Health* (Grand Rapids, MI: Baker Books, 2013).

a lot about Becca's character. A compelling vision is a "yes" to one thing and a "no" to anything that competes with it.

A vision without a strategy/plan is just wishing, so the final part of the process is crafting a strategy to fulfill the family vision. The family's strategy answers the question, "How do we get there?" This aspect is even more specific, with clear goals, a timeline, and an analysis of the resources needed to reach the goals. Remember, you can't build what you can't see.

> *The only thing worse than being blind is having sight but no vision.*
> —Helen Keller[17]

THE POWER OF VISION

Monty Roberts tells a story that demonstrates the power of vision. He became a world-renowned expert on horse training, but not without some serious challenges along the way. During Monty's senior year in high school, one of his teachers, Mr. Fowler, gave an assignment. He instructed his students to write a paper titled "My Goals in Life," detailing what they envisioned for themselves. He told them, "It should be like painting a picture of your lives in the future, as if all your ambitions had been realized." But Mr. Fowler added a caveat: "This vision should be realistic. I don't want to hear about some crazy, off-the-wall plan."

Monty's father was a horse trainer, and Monty had been around horses all his young life. Since age nine, he had been drawing stables and training facilities. He confidently turned in a paper to Mr. Fowler with a detailed plan to build a thoroughbred racehorse facility. He was stunned five days later when his paper was returned with a big red F at the top. When he took his paper to Mr. Fowler, his teacher justified the grade because he felt Monty had ignored his instructions to be realistic. He knew Monty didn't come from a wealthy family and told him, "It's a wild, unattainable

---
17 Helen Keller, et al., *The Story of My Life* (Minneola, NY: Dover, 1996).

dream." But he gave Monty the opportunity to revise his paper and turn it in again to avoid a failing grade.

After seeing Monty struggle for several days with this assignment, his mother offered her support. She told him if he thought it was an unattainable dream, he should change his paper. But if he really believed he could accomplish his goal, he should just resubmit the paper with no changes and live with the consequences. That's what he did. He turned his paper back in along with a note telling Mr. Fowler that he could grade the paper as he wished, but he had no right to limit his aspirations. Monty never found out what he made on that paper, but when grades were mailed out at the end of the year, he had made an A in the class.[18]

Monty went on to achieve his goals and established Flag Is Up Farms, a sprawling ranch (very much like the one he had described in high school) in Solvang, California, devoted to the care and training of thoroughbred horses. Many years after his high school graduation, he received an unexpected call from Mr. Fowler, who had retired and was the social director of his church group. He wanted to know if he could bring out a group of seniors to tour Monty's ranch, so Monty arranged a time.

When the bus arrived, Mr. Fowler was the first one off and greeted Monty warmly. Many of the older members of the group weren't very mobile and needed to view the facility from the bus, but Monty had ensured that plenty of horses were training nearby for them to see. After the tour, Mr. Fowler publicly acknowledged that although he had been Monty's teacher, Monty had taught him an important lesson: "A teacher does not have the right to put a cap on the aspirations of his students, no matter how unreal those aspirations might seem."[19]

Monty's vision had been strong enough to endure inaccurate criticism, even from an early age. It was what gave him direction and passion. When your family establishes a vision and commits to it, the vision will become

---

18 Monty Roberts, *The Man Who Listens to Horses* (Toronto: Vintage Canada, 1998) 98-100.
19 Monty Roberts, *The Man Who Listens to Horses*, 176-178.

an anchor that provides stability to withstand the pressures, heartaches, and criticism we all suffer from time to time.

NOT ONLY DIRECTION, BUT REDIRECTION

Because mission and vision provide ongoing direction, they are invaluable during those times when we temporarily lose our focus or stray from our intended path—in other words, when we drift. They don't just start us down the right road; they help us find our way back when we get turned around. All families—ours included—get off track from time to time, sometimes quite literally.

A few years ago, all of my (Michelle's) extended family vacationed together in Steamboat Springs, Colorado. It was a collection of nieces, nephews, kids, and grandkids—a whole army of people. We stayed in a beautiful location, and one day everybody loaded up in the cars and drove to a spot where we started a long climb up a mountain. By the time we got to the top and had taken in the magnificent scenery, we were tired. Almost everyone decided to take the gondola back down, but Rodney and I had heard there was a walking trail down to the base of the mountain that was only about a three-mile hike. We figured that wouldn't be a problem, so we and our daughter Ashlyn decided to walk back down. We waved to the rest of the family as they descended in the gondola, and we started down the trail.

Along the trek, we noticed our path led us away from the overhead gondola. We assumed it wasn't a big deal. We were sure we'd come out next to the bottom terminal of the gondola. Wrong. When we arrived at the base of the mountain, we discovered we were five miles away from where we had intended to be! Several hours later, when we finally caught up with the rest of the family, we were completely exhausted! The next day, Rodney, Ashlyn, and I were reminded of our long detour as we felt our muscle cramps and sore ankles. I learned an important lesson through that experience: Even though we had gotten way off course, the reason we were able to get back on track was that we knew our ultimate destination.

A lot of people like to quote Jeremiah 29:11: "'For I know the plans I have for you,' declares the Lord, 'plans to prosper you and not to harm you, plans to give you hope and a future.'" It's a wonderful promise. Who wouldn't want this kind of assurance from God? But what many people don't realize is that this promise came at perhaps the lowest point in Israel's long history—and they'd had several low points! Jeremiah was passing along God's message that because of the people's stubbornness and continued participation in idolatry, God was removing his blessing from them. Jerusalem, their cherished capital city, had been destroyed by the Babylonians. Their temple was leveled, and many of the people were taken to Babylon as captives, living in exile in a state of emotional and spiritual despair (read Psalm 137 to learn more of the Israelites' plight).

In the middle of their heartache, Jeremiah relayed God's promise that Babylon wasn't their *final* destination. They were enduring a time of struggle and disappointment, but God was still in charge. They had wandered off track and were suffering for it, but their dismal times would come to an end. Someday, they would return to their homeland. Jeremiah was urging his people to start with the end in mind. It was a message that was hard for them to hear, but it would help them endure. And everything happened just as God had said.

> *The way we choose to get to where we're going defines what it's going to be like when we get there.*
> —Seth Godin[20]

---

20 Seth Godin, *"The Ends and the Means,"* Seth's Blog (blog), September 1, 2018, https://seths.blog/2018/09/the-ends-and-the-means/.

FIRST STEP, NEXT STEP

The first step in getting to where you want to be as a family is *knowing* where you want to go as a family, which is why a mission statement and vision statement are essential. So for now, put your time and effort into analyzing, dreaming, discussing, praying over, and creating your family mission and vision statements. Before you go any further in this process, you need to have the end in mind. Drift isn't inevitable . . . at least, not for long. If you invest in identifying your family's purpose and direction, you'll be on the right path, and when you realize you're drifting, you'll know how to get back on track.

In our role in working with all kinds of families, we often try to imagine what it would be like if everyone in our homes, churches, and communities stopped resisting what God has shown is best for them, and if they found meaning, joy, and fulfillment in following Him with all their hearts. What would the world look like if we quit being content with "survival mode" and instead committed to thriving in our relationships and spiritual growth? What if we all started living the "full" life God created us to experience?

Now, more than ever, we hear a lot of voices competing with our vision, our mission, our values, and ultimately the decisions we will make. We know there's a better way, and it saddens us because it's easier than most people think to make adjustments that will vastly improve the quality of their family life. We like to quote this insight: "Small tweaks will take you to giant peaks."[21] If there was ever a time for families to make the SHIFT, we believe it's now. Every family ends up somewhere. Is your family going wherever life takes you? Or are you going somewhere *on purpose*?

---

21 Ed Young, *The Creative Leader: Unleashing the Power of Your Creative Potential* (Nashville, B & H Publishing, 2006), 131.

THINK ABOUT IT:
1) Is your family currently most in need of passion, motivation, direction, or purpose? How do you plan to strengthen any weak areas?
2) At this stage in your life, what would be the value of your creating (or reviewing) a mission and vision statement for you or your family?
3) When is the best time for you to get started? (The sooner the better! Check the schedules of everyone who needs to be involved, and put it on your calendar.)
4) Do you anticipate any resistance? If you do, how will you handle it?
5) Do you feel pressured to tightly control the process? If you do, how can you relax and invite people to participate in their own way?
6) How would you describe a family that's thriving? Can you give examples of families you know or examples of families in books you've read or the Bible?
7) How would you describe a family that is merely surviving?
8) How would you rate your own family: surviving, thriving, or somewhere in between? Explain your answer.

DO IT:
Answer and discuss these questions as a family:
1) Have your initial family conversation to get input about your mission and vision.
2) After you talk, write your first version down.

CHAPTER 3

GO!

COMMIT TO SOME PRACTICAL FIRST STEPS

---

*Your commitments can develop you or destroy you,
but either way, they will define you.*
—Rick Warren[22]

There are two kinds of people in this world—those who like jigsaw puzzles and those who don't. I (Rodney) fall into the camp of not liking jigsaw puzzles because they require too much time and patience. On the other hand, Michelle loves them. To her, sitting down and working on a puzzle is not only therapeutic but also a way to enjoy meaningful

---

22   Rick Warren, "Your Commitments Shape Your Life," *Crosswalk*, August 28, 2016, www.crosswalk.com/devotionals/daily-hope-with-rick-warren/daily-hope-with-rick-warren-august-28-2016.html#:~:text=Your%20commitments%20shape%20your%20life%20more%20than%20anything,years%2C%20because%20we%20become%20whatever%20we%E2%80%99re%20committed%20to.

conversation. Working on a puzzle with someone or as a family allows you to work toward a common goal.

Have you ever stopped to think about what the most important part of a puzzle is? It's not any certain puzzle piece, but without this one critical component, you almost certainly wouldn't be able to complete the puzzle. Curious as to what it is? It's the box top! Without having a clear picture of what you're attempting to put together, working on a puzzle can become one of the most frustrating experiences of your life. Even if you get lucky in finding a few pieces to fit together, over time, you'll probably end up throwing in the towel and quitting. The puzzle will be incomplete.

That is a picture of how most people live their lives—they try to put the pieces together without even knowing what their life, marriage, or family is supposed to look like. In the previous chapters, we discussed the importance of having a clear mission and vision and how these keep us from drifting in our most important relationships. When we have a clear picture of what that is and why it is important, it can change the trajectory of individuals, marriages, families, and generations to come. But having the "box top" doesn't necessarily mean that the puzzle is going to be a piece of cake. Putting hundreds or even thousands of puzzle pieces together still requires patience, focus, communication, and teamwork. Still, knowing your "box top" picture and what you're wanting to accomplish can make all the difference in the world. A clear picture of your mission and vision (your "why") will motivate what you do as you strive to fulfill God's plans and purposes for your life and family.

> *A goal is not about what you accomplish. It's about what you become.*
> —Michael Hyatt[23]

---

23 Michael Hyatt, "Is Your Goal Challenging or Just Crazy? Here's How to Tell the Difference," *Full Focus*, January 2, 2015, fullfocus.co/challenging-or-just-crazy/.

TAILORED MOTIVATION

Each member of our families may have very different fuels of motivation to keep them going. Some are inspired by encouragement and recognition, and others find inspiration in the immensity of the challenge. The thought of a far-future benefit gets some engines revving, and others prefer when they can envision immediate gain. Some desire the prospect of personal advancement, and for others, the opportunity to have an impact far beyond themselves is what matters most. This point may surprise you: Some of the people joining you on this journey to stop the drift are probably not exactly like you, and they don't think exactly like you do! If you try to force square pegs into your round hole of motivation, all will be frustrated, and at least one of you will probably quit. And even one person not being involved in the family's purpose is a huge downer; all the empty spaces need to be put together to complete the picture.

The first task of any communicator is to know your audience. Yes, the person sleeping next to you and the ones who are in bed down the hall are your audience for your "vision talk." The question is, do you know what captures the minds and hearts of each person? Can you tell when their eyes glaze over and when they sit up with anticipation? Have you learned what deflates each one and what makes each feel inspired and energized? If you can't answer those questions, it's not a hopeless situation. You just need to talk and listen more than ever to your family members during this process of crafting your mission and vision. Remember, opposites attract . . . and too often, opposites attack!

A wise person has the ability to enter other people's worlds—to understand what they value, how they think, how long they take to make decisions, and what makes their eyes light up. Presentation is everything. It's just not what you say and how you say it; it's also when you say it that can make all the difference. Many years ago, we (Rodney and Michelle) made a bold decision to announce to our families that we would no longer be traveling to Dallas on Christmas Day like we had been doing each year since we moved to Florida. We wanted our children to wake up on Christmas and experience it in our home so that we could establish our own traditions and memories around our Christmas tree. I (Michelle) knew this was going to be a tough sell, and it wouldn't go over very well with my side of the family. I delegated delivering the dreaded news to Rodney because I knew it would be too awkward and emotional for me to share our intentions with my parents, three sisters, and their families. I also knew the timing would be extremely important to avoid any misunderstanding or dampen the mood over the holidays. Our plan was for Rodney to give them our decision a year in advance, on the last night of our usual Christmastime visit. I'll never forget that evening together with my family at my sister Kim's house. My parents, my sisters and brothers-in-law, our kids, and our nieces and nephews were gathered in my sister's living room. Rodney spoke up and said he had an announcement to make. You could see the curiosity on everyone's faces, as if we were getting ready to make an exciting announcement, like we were expecting a baby or maybe moving back to Dallas. When Rodney had everyone's attention, he told them, "Everyone, this is the last Christmas we'll be coming to Dallas." You could have heard a pin drop. Faces displayed confusion, shock, and disbelief. Then all of a sudden, my youngest sister, Heather, broke out in tears and said, "You mean to tell us that our children will never know your children for the rest of their lives?" Rodney was suddenly sitting in the hot seat. Everyone glared at him as if he could be executed by a firing squad of harsh looks. After the tears and drama subsided, we were finally able to explain ourselves. We shared our hopes and dreams for our family and our desire to make memories and establish traditions of our own. It was a tough conversation, but it was worth it. We had charted a course for our three children, and we had communicated our vision to my family so they would understand—maybe not agree, but at least understand.

Once the dust settled from our big announcement, one of my brothers-in-law approached Rodney and said, "Bro, that took some guts! I've been wanting to say that for a long time, but I didn't have the courage to do it. I was afraid of being put on the family blacklist ... like what just happened to you!" As Rodney learned firsthand from delivering his big "vision talk" to my family, it's vitally important to know your audience and be aware of how each person is wired as you talk through and implement your plans for the future. You will want to clearly share the benefits to each member of the family before you unveil the process. If we move to the process (the actual steps to accomplish the goals) too quickly, we run the risk of creating resistance among those who need their hearts engaged before they can put their hands to the task. John C. Maxwell reminds us that when it comes to leveraging influence, "leaders touch a heart before they ask for a hand."[24]

> *Presentation is everything. It's not just* what *you say and* how *you say it; it's also* when *you say it that can make all the difference.*
> —Rodney and Michelle Gage

Let us make a recommendation: Early in the conversations about mission and vision, take time to invite your spouse and kids to dream big. This inspires everyone to envision what could be and should be. God has made us to dream. Here are some statements that invite more discussion:
- Imagine what it would look like if our marriage (or family) lived for something far greater than ourselves! What do you think that purpose might be?
- Imagine the impact we can have on people in our family, in the neighborhood, at school, and at work! How do you envision people being affected by us?

---
[24] John C. Maxwell, *The 21 Indispensable Qualities of a Leader: Becoming the Person Others Will Want to Follow* (Nashville: Thomas Nelson, 1999).

- Imagine what our marriage (or family) will look like a year from now, in five years, and in ten years if we keep living for this purpose? What do you think we'll need to keep us going?

And as you read this, how do you imagine these conversations going? What excites you about the prospect of engaging the people you love to uncover God's purposes for you and find His path to accomplish them? You need plenty of motivation too!

> *You can start from where you are with what you've got and go to where it is you want to go.*
> —Zig Ziglar[25]

CRAFTING

So far, we've asked you to think, pray, talk, and write out your mission and vision. We didn't expect this to take just one talk. It's a process of interaction, careful listening, reframing ideas, listening some more, and finding what inspires each person. But at some point—maybe now—it's time to craft these statements.

Be sure to write down your mission and vision statements. Don't let them just hang in the air. If it's not on paper, it's just a vapor! Sources as widely diverse as the Bible and university studies show the impact of writing down what we want to achieve. About four hundred years before Christ was born, the prophet Habakkuk recorded God's directive:

> *Then the LORD replied: "Write down the revelation and make it plain on tablets so that a herald may run with it. For the revelation awaits an appointed time; it speaks of the end and will not prove false. Though it linger, wait for it; it will certainly come and will not delay."* —Habakkuk 2:2-3

---

25 Zig Ziglar, *Born to Win: Find Your Success Code* (Issaquah, WA: Made for Success, 2017).

A study several years ago by Harvard found that the 3 percent of those who graduated with MBAs and wrote down their goals earned *ten times more* than the other 97 percent combined.[26] And Dr. Gail Matthews of the Dominican University in California reports that of 267 graduates, the 76 percent who wrote their goals (not only about their hoped-for earnings) and shared them with others accomplished them. Matthews states, "My study provides empirical evidence for the effectiveness of three coaching tools: accountability, commitment, and writing down one's goals."[27]

Writing your statements as a couple or a family has several benefits:
- It will force you to clarify your purpose and direction.
- It will lead to clear, actionable first steps.
- It will give you motivation to act.
- It will help you say "no" to good opportunities, so you can say "yes" to the best ones.
- It will help you overcome apathy and resistance.
- It will give you a clear understanding of the progress you make, so you can celebrate each step.

> *Figure out who you are and do it on purpose.*
> —Dolly Parton[28]

ROAD SIGNS

Since finding and fulfilling God's design for your family is a journey, you'll need road signs along the way. Many companies put inspiring quotes in frames to hang in offices and halls. And is there a teenager who doesn't have

---

26   Sid Savara, "Why 3% of Harvard MBAs Make Ten Times as Much as the Other 97% Combined," *Sid Savara*, https://sidsavara.com/why-3-of-harvard-mbas-make-ten-times-as-much-as-the-other-97-combined/.

27   Sarah Gardner and Dave Albee, "Study focuses on strategies for achieving goals, resolutions," *Dominican University of California*, February 1, 2015, archived at https://web.archive.org/web/20200115170659/http://www.dominican.edu/dominicannews/study-highlights-strategies-for-achieving-goals.

28   @DollyParton (Dolly Parton), "Figure out who you are and do it on purpose," *Twitter*, April 8, 2015, 3:40 p.m., https://x.com/DollyParton/status/585890099583397888/photo/1.

a poster or screen saver of a band or athlete in the bedroom? We put these up to encourage us and to remind us of what's most important, and I dare say, the things those quotes and posters advertise aren't nearly as important as your mission and vision statements for your marriage and family.

Put your family vision, mission, and purpose statements in visible areas throughout your home so everyone can see them each day. That's just the first step. Refer to them often to reinforce their meaning. Discuss how you may have gotten off track and how you've come back to the path. I suggest you tell your spouse and kids that you want to engage them by talking about the statements on a regular basis. It could be over a pizza or at your favorite burger joint or ice cream parlor or at Saturday morning breakfast—the location is far less important than the intention to have quality conversations. The purpose for talking about the mission and vision often is to keep the "box top" in front of your family at all times.

A friend of ours did this with his wife and high school–aged son. He explained, "Every night for the next month, I want us to talk—just for a few minutes—about our commitment to our purpose." It took some thought and preparation, but for the next week, he led them in discussions of passages from the Bible (like the ones in this book) and questions about how God wants them to live out their purpose in light of pressures like busy schedules, cultural temptations, and relationships with friends. Finally, he asked them to weigh in vulnerably and honestly about how their purpose shaped their responses to victories and defeats, encouragement and criticism. When the month was over, he said, "When I started, I was pretty sure my wife was on board, but my son . . . I wasn't sure at all. But I didn't preach to him. I talked about what I was learning about a host of topics, and I asked him what he thought. When I disagreed, I tried really hard to avoid shutting down the conversation. Instead, I said, 'Tell me more about what you're thinking.' It was far better than anything I had imagined! In fact, I look back on those conversations as the launching pad for more meaningful talks about all kinds of issues since then." What this father did with his son is what we pray will take place in your marriage and family. He decided to stop the drift and take the necessary steps to make the shift.

> *The purpose for talking about the mission and vision often is to keep the "box-top" in front of your family at all times.*
> —Rodney and Michelle Gage

NEHEMIAH PRINCIPLE

There is a great principle in the Bible known as the Nehemiah principle. Nehemiah mobilized a remnant of people to rebuild the walls of Jerusalem, which had been destroyed by previous invasions. Without the protection of the walls, the Jews living in Jerusalem were left vulnerable to other attacks, so Nehemiah led the charge to restore them in just fifty-two days. At day twenty-six, when the walls reached half their original height, the workers' strength began to give out. They struggled against threats of attack, low morale, and doubt that the wall would actually protect their loved ones. Nehemiah stepped in to rally the builders together, recast vision, and remind them of the greater purpose they were working toward. He posted soldiers at exposed places along the walls and stationed them next to family homes. Then Nehemiah offered this reassurance to the people: "Don't be afraid of them. Remember the Lord, who is great and awesome, and fight for your families, your sons and your daughters, your wives and your homes" (Nehemiah 4:14).

You can use the Nehemiah principle to refresh your vision every twenty-six days, or maybe it's easier to schedule a refresh conversation with your family once a month. Don't miss this. The distractions and temptations for more upgrades and experiences from our culture never stop. There's a constant pressure to value success, pleasure, and approval more than God and His purposes. It's not that these things are wrong.

If they're gifts from God, we can enjoy them and use them as resources. When we have this perspective, success, pleasure, and approval are our servants ... but they make lousy masters! How often do you need to hear your spouse say, "I love you"? How often do your kids need to hear, "I'm so proud of you"? If our hearts are truly captured by God's purpose to make a difference in everything we say and do, we'll talk about it all the time! Especially to the people who matter most in our lives. Remember, what you love the most is what you talk about the most. Your spouse and children need to be reminded of the love, acceptance, support, belief, and confidence you have in them. No one ever died from receiving too much encouragement or hope. There will always be challenges, distractions, and setbacks along the way. However, our love and commitment to each other must be reinforced over and over. You may be in a single family or blended family and currently feel powerless to lead your children or step-children in a way they need to go. We (Rodney and Michelle) want you to know that we believe in you and your family, and we have no doubt that God has you right where you are for such a time as this. Your sons or daughters or stepsons or stepdaughters need to know that they are loved and that God has a great plan and purpose for their lives.

LIVE IT OUT

Every new habit takes practice ... and plenty of trial and error. As we change (or at least clarify) the direction of our marriage and family, we need to take practical steps. Each step reinforces our commitment to take the next one, and before long, a new set of habits takes shape.

Let us suggest a few steps you might want to take as you make God's mission and vision real in your experience:

1) **Start small.**

If you aren't reading the Bible, commit to taking a few minutes at the beginning of each day to refocus your mind, heart, and perspective on what matters most to help you live with greater intention. I highly recommend something like the *One Year Bible,* or check out the large variety of Bible readings and devotionals on the Bible App called YouVersion. We have a 40-day devotional on the YouVersion Bible App called "ReThink Life."

If you want to make prayer more of a priority, invest time in praying every day. I (Rodney) used to hear my dad say, "Much prayer, much power. Little prayer, little power. No prayer, no power!"

If you want to speak with more kindness to your spouse and kids, spend five minutes every day writing down what you appreciate about each of them. We suggest practicing these small disciplines in the morning to set the tone for your day. It also allows you to be proactive instead of reactive with your day and with each other.

2) **Keep the vision fresh.**

Over and over again, remind yourself—and those around you—of the benefits of fulfilling your mission and vision. Point to other couples or families you admire, ask about their motivation, and take encouragement from what they do right? One of the best ways to accomplish this is by reading or listening to other books, listening or watching *The Winning Podcast,* and attending conferences and retreats that are designed to strengthen marriage and family relationships. Remember, we reap what we sow. Sow into and invest in our marriage and family relationships.

3) **Tell others about your commitment.**

Your spouse and kids need to know that you're devoted to what you've all committed to be and do. Invite them to ask if you're being faithful to your commitment and share what you're learning. Let them hold you accountable and be a model for them.

4) **Enjoy the rewards.**

You've made this commitment because you believe God will use it and you to make a difference in the lives of others. From the beginning, as you take steps of faith, you'll see God answer your prayers and take you further toward your destiny. Enjoy every moment of the journey.

5) Don't give up.

There will be plenty of times when you fall short of your intentions. It's easy to get distracted, forget about or blow off your commitment, or slip back into old habits. We're all going to mess up and fail along the way. When we get lost on a road trip, it doesn't mean we turn around and go back home—and the same is true when you drift from your mission and vision. We just have to identify where we are, revisit where we're trying to go, and get back on the right track that will lead us to our destination.

To make a SHIFT, we must first take strategic steps to turn our initial commitments into established habits. The good news is that it doesn't take long for a new habit to form in our minds, hearts, and behaviors. Don't wait any longer. Identify the steps you want to take . . . and take them!

THINK ABOUT IT:

1) Describe what motivates (and what demotivates) each person who is part of your mission and vision as a family.
2) How do you need to tailor your communication to inspire each one?
3) Why is it important to "sell" the benefits before unveiling the process?
4) What are a few very practical steps you can take to fulfill your mission and vision?
5) Do you think it's necessary for you to remind yourself and others to stay on track? Why or why not?
6) What steps will you take today?

DO IT:

Answer and discuss these questions as a family:

1) Have another conversation or two with your spouse and family about your mission and vision to make both of the statements clear and strong.
2) Write these statements in their (hopefully) final form.
3) Post them in a prominent place in your house.

STEP 2

HOLD TO CORE VALUES

A SHIFT IN FOCUS

CHAPTER 4

FAMILY IS A TEAM SPORT

STRENGTHEN YOUR FAMILY "TEAM"

If you're going to play together as a team, you got to care for one another. You got to love each other.
—Vince Lombardi[29]

My (Michelle's) parents came to Orlando to visit us a few years ago, and we wanted to take them canoeing in an original Florida habitat called Wekiwa Springs. We wanted them to see what Central Florida looked like before concrete covered so much of it, and we were excited to take them for a close-up look at manatees and alligators. Our three kids were in a canoe, my parents went together, and Rodney and I jumped

---

29 Peter Economy, "17 Inspiring Quotes About the Remarkable Power of Teamwork," *Inc.*, October 11, 2018, https://www.inc.com/peter-economy/17-inspiring-quotes-about-remarkable-power-of-teamwork.html.

in one. A few minutes later, the other two canoes were out of sight, but Rodney and I had barely budged. It wasn't for a lack of trying—but we were paddling in opposite directions! Instead of working with each other, we were working against each other. We kept spinning around and around very slowly, but we weren't making any progress. Paddling harder didn't work. We had to find another solution, or we'd still be there today. Finally, we talked about the problem and found a solution, so we could paddle in tandem and catch up with the others. Canoeing requires two things every family needs: strength and synchrony. When we align our efforts with others in the family, wonderful things can happen. Without that alignment, we get stuck and frustrated.

Alignment with others in the family is essential. In the North, drivers complain of potholes. Down here in Central Florida, we laugh at those small holes in the road. We have sinkholes that can swallow cars and whole houses entirely! Potholes, our northern friends tell us, can cause significant damage to a car, especially the alignment. But at least the driver still has their car! Though, after hearing of a friend who hit a pothole and the serious damage it caused to their car, we had a lot of sympathy. When a driver doesn't see the hole in the road and hits it dead on, it can . . . well, I (Rodney) am not really sure what happens in the dark recesses under a car. To find out, I went to the source—the Firestone website. It explains:

> *Alignment is a really complex topic covering a variety of terms and a smorgasbord of parts. When your wheels are out of alignment, your tires aren't pointing in the right direction. This will affect your steering and suspension, but more importantly, it could affect your safety and the durability of your tires and all the parts controlling them.*[30]

---

[30] "Everything You Need to Know about Wheel Alignment," Firestone, August 22, 2016, https://blog.firestonecompleteautocare.com/alignment/everything-you-need-to-know-about-wheel-alignment/.

Even a slight misalignment in the tires can cause a car to drift to the right or the left. If it moves to the right, you'll hit the bumps on the side of the road to warn you to correct your path. But if you drift to the left, you might hit oncoming traffic, with disastrous results. Even if you don't have a wreck, the misalignment will wear out your tires more quickly, and it'll cost more money.

A lot of families have drifted out of alignment. Each person may have different values, or more often, two or more people form alliances against others in the family. Each side is sure they're right, so as arguments inevitably happen, each side becomes more entrenched. Instead of trying to work with each other, they are working against each other.

Les and Leslie Parrott are psychologists who are considered two of the nation's leading experts on marriage. In an article called "The Secret of Growing Together," they write:

> *An enduring marriage requires possibility thinking, elasticity, and resilience. It needs continual attention and adaptation to grow together. It requires a shift in interests as our partner's interests shift. In other words, to remain good and strong, marriage entails a lifelong project of adjusting and readjusting our attitudes. For this is the only path to finding positive options to our most perplexing circumstances.*[31]

No family is beyond hope, but all of us need to follow the Parrott's advice to "find positive options," no matter how far we've drifted apart.

> *The farthest distance between two people is misunderstanding.*
> — Rodney and Michelle Gage

Most family psychologists believe that there are four common parenting styles: permissive, uninvolved, authoritarian, and authoritative.

---
31 Drs. Les and Leslie Parrott, "The Secret to Growing Together," *Les and Leslie Parrott*, August 20, 2013, https://www.lesandleslie.com/devotions/the-secret-to-growing-together/.

These styles, though, aren't limited to parents and kids. We see them in marriages, at work, and in friendships.

- *Permissive* spouses and parents have rules, but they don't enforce them. They may yell, but they don't administer the consequences they've promised would be the result of misbehavior. They claim to be loving and forgiving, and they're susceptible to tears and pleas.
- *Uninvolved* spouses and parents provide little if any time, attention, instructions, love, or guidance. Some of these people are simply repeating the example they saw in their parents, and others are so overwhelmed by traumatic life events that they have nothing left to give.
- *Authoritarian* spouses and parents are strict and demanding. What matters is obedience, blind obedience. They don't value others' opinions, and they don't connect with their feelings. From the outside, the marriage or family may look very "put together," but it's put together with fear, not love.
- *Authoritative* spouses and parents are servant leaders. They have a sense of intention and purpose, and they lovingly and patiently take the rest of the family with them. They have rules, and they let people experience the consequences of their choices, both good and bad. They invest time and energy to build strong relationships, and they value each person's uniqueness.

BENCHMARKS

In the chart in chapter 2, we looked at the relationship between mission, values, vision, and strategy. Now, it's time to focus on values and ask the question, "What do we care about?" Or another way of asking is, "What are the non-negotiable qualities our family is committed to live by? And what are the intangibles that will set our family apart and foster success for each member of the family?"

Stated values aren't as important as values we live out. In fact, if there's no coherence between what we say is important and how we act, we send a loud and clear message that we're pretenders. That's painful to write, and we're sure it's painful to read, but it's true.

The Bible is a rich treasure trove about what matters to God and, therefore, what should matter to us. Let us share two passages that communicate God's values loudly and clearly. Jeremiah was called "the Weeping Prophet" because God often gave him such painful things to tell people who weren't following God's path. It's human nature to get our identity from our culture's values, but Jeremiah says there's a better source:

This is what the LORD says:
"Let not the wise boast of their wisdom
or the strong boast of their strength
or the rich boast of their riches,
but let the one who boasts boast about this:
that they have the understanding to know me,
that I am the LORD, who exercises kindness,
justice and righteousness on earth,
for in these I delight,"
declares the LORD. —Jeremiah 9:23-24

What does it mean to boast? A "boast" is what's most important to us. Have you ever thought about what people living in today's culture like to boast about? Their intelligence, their power, their wealth, and their possessions. These values are supreme in the culture around us, and God warns they're common in many of us too. At the end of the day, what matters most in life is knowing God and making Him known to those around us. We were made by God and for God, and until we understand that fact, life will never make sense. God wants us to place our trust in Him and to align our values with His: kindness, justice, righteousness, and grace. That's what's most important to God, and as we follow Him, these values become most important to us too. Romans 12:2 reminds us to challenge the norm of our culture: "Stop imitating the ideals and opinions of the culture around you, but be inwardly transformed by the Holy Spirit through a total reformation of how you think. This will empower you to discern God's will as you live a beautiful life, satisfying and perfect in his eyes" (TPT). Does it matter whether we have our culture's values or God's? Isn't it a lot easier just to go with the flow? It may be easier, but it's deadly. All of us have something that's supremely important to us, something that's worth more than anything. That's why the Old English word to describe our stated value of God is worth-ship. When anything or anyone is most important, it becomes an object of our devotion; we invest our energy and time into it, and we expect it to make our lives full and meaningful. In his Kenyon College commencement speech, novelist David Foster Wallace warned the students and their parents:

If you worship money and things—if they are where you tap real meaning in life—then you will never have enough. Never feel you have enough. It's the truth. Worship your own body and beauty and sexual allure and you will always feel ugly. . . . Worship power—you feel weak and afraid, and you will need even more power over others to keep the fear at bay. Worship your intellect, being seen as smart—you will end up feeling stupid, a fraud, always on the verge of being found out. The insidious thing about these forms of worship is not that they're evil or sinful; it is that they are unconscious. They are default settings.

Money, possessions, intelligence, influence, beauty, and power aren't necessarily wrong, but they'll cause us to drift if they become our highest values and pursuits. They simply can't give us what we long for. They're our "default settings," so unless something radically shifts our values, they stay at the top of our priority lists. Having a real, authentic relationship with God is far better.

A second Scripture passage gives another glimpse of God's values that he wants us to embrace. King David wrote many psalms. They range from the loftiest praise to complaints that God hadn't come through like he expected. But even when David was discouraged, he kept praying and seeking God. He often described his love for God and his commitment to value what God values. In Psalm 15, he wrote:

Lord, who dares to dwell with you?
Who presumes the privilege of being close to you,
living next to you in your shining place of glory?
They are passionate and wholehearted,
always sincere and always speaking the truth—
for their hearts are trustworthy.
They refuse to slander or insult others;
they'll never listen to gossip or rumors,
nor would they ever harm another with their words.
They will despise evil and evil workers
while commending the faithful ones who follow after the truth.
They make firm commitments and follow through,
even at great cost.
They never crush others with exploitation
and they would never be bought with a bribe
against the innocent.
Those who do these things will never be shaken; they will stand firm
forever. —Psalm 15:1-5 (TPT)

David valued God's truth, so his words reflected truth he had hidden in his heart about God. David valued kindness, so he treated each person according to the Golden Rule. He valued honesty, so he kept his word even when it wasn't pleasant or convenient. And he valued justice, so he cared for the poor and refused to engage in shady business deals.

Let's be honest: We may aspire to these qualities, but none of us has arrived. Even the most humble, the most committed, and the most mature still wrestle with flaws and temptations.

> *The goal isn't perfection, it's progress.*
> —Rodney and Michelle Gage

God's promised outcome if we practice His values is in the last line of the psalm: Those who practice these values "will never be shaken." In other words, no matter what tragedies we endure, and no matter how much chaos is going on around us, we have God's promises as "an anchor for the soul." We'll have confidence that when everything around us looks out of control, God is still sovereign over it all.

Years ago, I (Rodney) wanted to do something for my son Luke that would mark a significant milestone in his life as he transitioned from boyhood to manhood. Luke was turning thirteen, so I reached out to some close friends who had served as key influences in his life, along with some of his closest friends. I also invited my father-in-law to fly into Orlando to participate. I planned a fun and special evening for Luke. We went to the house of a friend who lived in the country. We cooked out, rode four-wheelers, shot guns, and built a big bonfire. Needless to say, it was a night filled with testosterone! As we approached the end of the evening, I invited Luke to sit in a chair in the middle of a circle. I had asked each of the seven men I had invited to prepare a two-minute talk about one of our family's seven core values. Each one affirmed Luke and shared the significance of the value. They challenged Luke to not only embrace that virtue but to live it out all the days of his life. Then Luke's friends stood up and each gave Luke kind words of affirmation, sharing how much they cherished their friendship with him. As we concluded the ceremony, my father-in-law gave Luke a ring that symbolized the love and legacy of our family. It was truly a moving and memorable moment to hear each man share their words of affirmation with Luke. I then stood up and read several verses from the Bible:

Luke 2:52 (NLT, author additions): "Jesus grew in wisdom (mentally) and in stature (physical) and in favor with God (spiritually) and all the people (relationally)."

First Corinthians 13:11 (NLT): "When I was a child, I spoke and thought and reasoned as a child. But when I grew up, I put away childish things."

After I read these verses to Luke, I shared this blessing over his life: Numbers 6:24 (TLB): "May the LORD bless and protect you; may the LORD's face radiate with joy because of you; may he be gracious to you, show you his favor, and give you his peace."

I wanted this evening to be a night Luke would never forget as he transitioned into the next season of his life as a man. It was important to reinforce the values that would guide his choices as he entered into middle school and high school. Knowing all that he would hear, see, and experience during those critical years, I wanted him to be reminded of our mission, vision, and values as a family. I wanted our values and the life principles spoken over him that night to inspire him and remind him to stand strong during his adolescent years. I also wanted to reassure him that our family values and God's promises would serve as an anchor in his life. It was truly an evening we will never forget. As parents, we have an incredible opportunity and responsibility given to us by God to shape the identities and values of our children. It doesn't guarantee that they won't fall into temptation or make bad choices as they grow older, but it does give them a spiritual and moral compass to know what is most important and who the source of truth is for our lives.

THE POWER OF REGRET

Not everyone has had the opportunity to grow up in a family where strong Christian values were taught and lived out. Michelle and I realize that the strength and depth of our childhood experiences are rare today. Perhaps the family you grew up in was anything but a Christian family.

Maybe you had to endure the pain of your parents' divorce or face the challenge of being raised in a single-parent home. Maybe you grew up in a blended family where there were conflicting views about what was really important. As a parent, maybe you missed opportunities that you wish you could get back with your kids. The truth is, all of us have made mistakes, and all of us have been wounded. We've all done things that we wish we had never done. All of us have hurt people we care about. And all of us wish we'd done something different in all these situations. In other words, to some degree, we're haunted by regret. The values we're trying to clarify and live by in our marriages and families today aren't dropped into an empty bucket. The bucket has a lot of other stuff in it, including some stuff that doesn't mesh very well with God's values. Regrets are part of being human. In his book *Your Best Year Ever*, Michael Hyatt observes, "The only people with no hope are those with no regrets."[32] In other words, if we don't care about anything, our failures won't bother us. But if we care, we'll be aware that we haven't lived up to our standards and even more, to God's standards.

Not long ago, I (Michelle), woke up in the middle of the night with tremendous pain in my shoulder and arm. I thought the pain was a result of sleeping awkwardly. The pain progressively got worse. After several days of discomfort, I finally went to the doctor to get evaluated. I underwent a series of X-rays and an MRI, and I even convinced Rodney to purchase a new mattress, but I was still living with pain in my shoulder. The results from my MRI showed that I had something called adhesive capsulitis. It's a condition more commonly referred to as frozen shoulder. It generally takes time and intense physical therapy for the condition to go away—unfortunately, there's no quick fix.

I learned the hard way that pain can serve as a tremendous indicator that something is wrong in our lives, and it can stick with us for some time. As long as we acknowledge our pain and do something about it,

---

32 Michael Hyatt, *Your Best Year Ever* (Grand Rapids, MI: Baker Books, 2018), 86.

we can overcome it. Pain can birth something positive if we'll let it. Let time be your friend and don't rush things—the best things take time. Regret isn't the worst thing in the world. It certainly can crush a person with a sense of worthlessness and helplessness, but if we let it, it can be a powerful fuel for growth. The problem is that we hate the feeling so much we often fail to acknowledge it, and if we don't acknowledge it, regret will eat us alive from the inside out.

WRITE THEM DOWN

If we don't write things down, our convictions easily evaporate into thin air. Starting right now, it's time to define what is important to you. It's time to write down your values. If you're single, spend some time reflecting on what's most important to you. If you're married, set aside some time to discuss the values that are most important to you as a couple and the values that you want to pass along to your children. If you already have kids, let them participate if they're old enough. You can call your list of values whatever you want: your family creed, code, or values. The main thing is to get them in writing. Leadership expert Craig Groeschel gives us encouragement and a warning: "If everything is important, nothing is important. If you value everything, you don't value anything."[33] He recommends a couple, a family, or a company have no more than ten stated values.

A number of years ago, we sat down and identified what we felt was most important to us. Most of the virtues that we were exposed to growing up had made it a bit easier for us because of the positive influence they had on our lives. This exercise allowed us to be thankful for and appreciative of the values taught in our homes. We took some time to write what was most important to us as a family. We confess that it was a bit of a challenge because we could identify many important things. The

---

33   Craig Groeschel, "Creating a Value-Driven Culture, Part 1," *Craig Groeschel Leadership Podcast*, March 3, 2016, https://open.life.church/training/343-craig-groeschel-leadership-podcast-creating-a-value-driven-culture-part-1.

hard part was narrowing our list down to less than ten. We went through multiple drafts and finally identified a list of values that we agreed were going to be the non-negotiables for our family. We sat down with our kids and shared what we believed captures God's heart for us the and our heart for Him.

GAGE FAMILY CORE VALUES

Honor is our choice.
Loyalty is our commitment.
Excellence is our spirit.
Faith is our foundation.
Purity is our heart.
Integrity is our standard.
Generosity is our way.
Attitude is everything.

These values are far more than words on a page. They serve as guidelines to direct us and guardrails to keep us from running into the ditch. We refer to them when we're making decisions, and they are the background music of our lives. They reinforce our *mission*, why we exist, and our *vision*, where we're going. We can't emphasize enough how incredibly important this exercise is for you and your family. If you don't have kids, this is a great opportunity to establish written values for your marriage. It's a big advantage to start now so that if or when you have children, you'll already have a moral "code" for your kids to live by. Perhaps you already have kids. Regardless of their age and stage, this exercise can be a game changer, but only if we live by them. It's one thing to have the values hanging on the wall—they have to be lived out down the hall.

Some parents assume they've lost their influence on their teenage children. That's not the case at all. They're still watching, still internalizing the values you're displaying through your words, attitudes, and actions. If you've done a good job imparting strong values to your kids, keep it up. If you've drifted from strong values in the past, as we stated earlier, you don't have to live with guilt or regret. Again, it's never too late to make the shift. We've seen God do amazing things in the lives of families when parents who have been authoritarian, permissive, or uninvolved have trusted God, made a major shift, and learned to love like Jesus loves. Strained marriages can be mended, distance can be bridged, pettiness can be overwhelmed by kindness, and bitterness can be turned into respect and love.

That's what you want, isn't it? We're sure it's the reason you're reading this book. A shift in values may be a minor mid-course correction, or it could be monumental. Either way, you can do it. Define your values, write them down, and own them. When it comes to casting vision, clarifying your mission, and identifying your core values as a family, we will say it, spray it, wheel it, and deal it until everyone in the family feels it!

THINK ABOUT IT:

1) What are some signs a marriage or a family is out of alignment?
2) How would you describe the traits and the impact of parents who are . . .
    - . . . permissive?
    - . . . uninvolved?
    - . . . authoritarian?
    - . . . and authoritative?
3) Which of the passages of Scripture in this chapter most powerfully captures your heart and reflects your values? Explain your answer.
4) What are some specific ways you can make a shift away from the world's values of beauty, intelligence, power, and money?
5) What did you learn about regret from Paul's letter to the Corinthians? Is your conscience screwed on too tight or too loose? How can you tell? (What would your spouse say about you?)

DO IT:

Answer and discuss these questions as a family:
1) It will take time to refine your list of values so you wholeheartedly commit to them, but for now, what are the words that describe your values?
2) Where is a place in the house where you can post your values, so everybody in the family will see them each day?
3) How do you want God to use these words in your life as well as in the lives of your spouse and your children?

CHAPTER 5

RULE BOOKS, PLAYBOOKS, AND THE GOOD BOOK

BUILD UNSHAKABLE VALUES

The number one influence on a child's life is not their peers, it's their parents
—Rodney Gage

Mathew Emmons is an expert American marksman. In the 2004 Summer Olympic Games in Athens, Greece, Matthew was on his way to winning his second gold medal. In fact, he was so far ahead of the competition that all he had to do was hit anywhere on the target. As Matthew took aim, like he always did, he aimed high at 12 o'clock and slowly lowered the barrel of his gun down until he took dead aim at the bull's eye. As he gently pulled the trigger, Matthew's shot hit the bullseye.

The crowd cheered, but suddenly, Matthew realized he had aimed at the wrong target! His mistake dropped him from first place to eighth and cost him a treasured gold medal. It happened because he was focused on the wrong target.

Sadly, that is a picture of many people in our culture today. When it comes to life, they're aiming at the wrong target. Many people are driven to climb the ladder to work their way to the top only to realize their ladder is leaning against the wrong wall. Most people don't know what they believe or why they believe it. Wrong has become right, and bad has become good. According to Barna Research:

More than four out of five adults – 83% – contend that they are concerned about the moral condition of the nation. Given that 84% of all adults consider themselves to be Christian, they have good reason to worry about the moral state of the country. In fact, many of their own views conflict with the moral teachings of their professed faith. Of the ten moral behaviors evaluated, a majority of Americans believed that three activities were "morally acceptable." Those included gambling (61%), co-habitation (60%), and sexual fantasies (59%). Nearly half of the adult population felt that two other behaviors were morally acceptable: having an abortion (45%) and having a sexual relationship with someone of the opposite sex other than their spouse (42%). About one-third of the population gave the stamp of approval to pornography (38%), profanity (36%), drunkenness (35%) and homosexual sex (30%). The activity that garnered the least support was using non-prescription drugs (17%).[34]

These statistics are reminiscent of a time in Israel's history when the nation didn't have a king. There was no leadership or moral authority to give direction and meaning to the people: "In those days there was no king in Israel. People did whatever they felt like doing" (Judges 17:6,

---

34 Barna Group, "Morality Continues to Decay," *Barna*, November 3, 2003, https://www.barna.com/research/morality-continues-to-decay/.

MSG). Now, thousands of years later, people in our culture still do "whatever they feel like doing."

According to Barna, the trends indicate that the moral perspectives of Americans are likely to continue to deteriorate:

> *Compared to surveys we conducted just two years ago, significantly more adults are depicting such behaviors as morally acceptable. For instance, there have been increases in the percentages that condone sexual activity with someone of the opposite gender other than a spouse, abortion (up by 25%), and a 20% jump in people's acceptance of "gay sex."*
>
> *The author of more than thirty books regarding faith and cultural trends, George Barna said that most people sense there's a problem, but they don't believe they contribute to it.*
>
> *Most of the people we interviewed believe that they are highly moral individuals and identify other people as responsible for the nation's moral decline. This is reflective of a nation where morality is generally defined according to one's feelings. In a postmodern society, where people do not acknowledge any moral absolutes, if a person feels justified in engaging in a specific behavior then they do not make a connection with the immoral nature of that action. Yet, deep inside, they sense that something is wrong in our society. They simply have not been able to put two and two together to recognize their personal liability regarding the moral condition of our nation.*[35]

As we can see, our culture and society have drifted from God's moral standard and original plan and purpose for our lives. Rather than submitting to God's leadership and authority, we've chosen to do whatever we feel like doing.

---

[35] Barna Group, "Morality Continues to Decay."

SOURCES OF VALUES

Have you ever stopped to think about what you really believe and why you believe it? Have you thought about what you value and why it is so important to you? More importantly, who influenced you to think like you think and believe what you believe? We didn't decide what's most important in a vacuum. A number of sources have shaped what we believe, what matters most, and who we want to become. The different sources may have varied impacts on individuals, but every person is affected by each of them in significant ways. Let's look at the most important ones.

Popular Culture

Our culture communicates values so powerfully and subtly that we seldom analyze them at all—we just soak them in without a moment's thought. Advertising reminds us of the things we don't have in their attempt to sell us on the things we think we need. Music influences our perspective on love and sex, and fashion is always a step ahead with the trends to make sure that what we wore yesterday is already out of style today. The hidden message in all this is: Whatever you have, it's not enough. We end up buying things we don't need with money we don't have to try and impress people we don't even like. People today are obsessed with happiness, but anxiety and depression are more common than ever. Why? Because the promise of happiness isn't found in bigger and better things.

This fact doesn't prevent us from believing that if we try hard enough, culture's promises will be fulfilled. We've become malleable consumers who are like kites in the wind, quickly darting wherever the wind blows us.

Unless we're perceptive and persistent in identifying the values we see and hear every day, the culture's values seep into every pore by osmosis.

> *You can't be an influencer if you're always being influenced.*
> —Levi Lusko[36]

Family Background

It's hard to overstate the impact of our experiences as children. Some of us are blessed to have grown up in secure, loving environments where people lived out Biblical principles and moral values for us. But most of us have encountered something less than that . . . and often much less. To the extent we've endured manipulation, emotional, physical, and sexual abuse, abandonment, or the craziness of living with an addict or alcoholic, the values we've absorbed are twisted by the pain and confusion we've internalized.

On the spectrum from mild to severe, most of us have been shaped by the wounds we experienced. In healthy families, people lie, they get hurt, and they feel angry, but they also have the heart to resolve these things before they take root in each person's soul. To the degree a family doesn't communicate love and support and isn't honest about the pain endured, people have one goal: survival. They play roles to make life work, avoid pain, and gain some kind of control over their lives. Some become rescuers who live to fix others' problems, and in these families, there are lots of problems! Others have concluded they can't trust anyone, so they withdraw, trying to become invisible in the hope that if no one notices them, they'll be safe from being hurt again. Still others have an opposite response to the same conclusion: They don't trust anyone, but for them, safety comes from intimidating, demanding, and controlling others with intellectual or physical power.

When couples stand at the altar, very few of them understand the powerful forces that have shaped the person standing next to them. For years after that moment, they wonder why in the world their spouse thinks, feels, and acts in that peculiar way! When one of them is pressed

---
36   Levi Lusko, "Finders Weepers, Losers Keepers" (speech, *Passion 2025*, Atlanta, GA, January 6, 2025).

to explain, the response is often, "I'm fine," which means, "Don't open Pandora's Box of all the pain I've spent my life trying to forget!"

In an article for Focus on the Family, Kay and Milan Yerkovich recount their struggle to uncover their past to resolve problems today, so they could have a much more loving, honest, and supportive tomorrow. They recall frequent and recurring communications that showed a much deeper problem:

> *Like many couples, we had a frustrating core pattern. For 15 years we did not understand this simple truth: Our marriage problems didn't start in our marriage. There were childhood wounds beneath our most irritating behaviors.*
>
> *A pattern of relating to others was set in motion long before each of us met our spouse. Our childhood experiences and the way our parents related to us have imprinted certain thought patterns and behaviors on us. . . .*
>
> *Being stuck in a hurtful core pattern for the first 15 years of our marriage was painful. We discovered that growth also brings challenges. It requires vulnerability to admit our brokenness. We had to break the destructive childhood patterns of relating that we both brought into our marriage.*
>
> *Our goal was to create the "secure connection" we missed out on as kids. Being a secure connector means becoming more like Christ, who gave and received love in healthy ways—honestly addressing problems with patience and understanding, repairing ruptures when they occurred. Couples with a secure connection are able to evaluate their strengths and weaknesses, own their contribution to relational difficulties and apologize sincerely when they make mistakes.*
>
> *As you consider how to address your love styles, remember this phrase: "Pick your pain." It's uncomfortable to grow and change; it's painful to remain stuck.*[37]

---

37 Kay and Milan Yerkovich, "How Childhood Experiences Impact Marriage Relationships," *Focus on the Family*, February 7, 2025, https://www.focusonthefamily.com/marriage/communication-and-conflict/how-childhood-experiences-impact-marriage-relationships.

Of course, the dysfunction, values and beliefs we carry into our marriages are also carried into our relationships with our kids. We may not treat our children exactly the same way our parents treated us. Instead of abusing them, we may smother them with attention and control, which produces its own set of problems for their future.

The point is very clear and often terribly disturbing: The problems we have with our spouse and children are usually the product of the values (good or bad) that were ingrained in us when we were children. These values shaped what we believe about love, security, honesty, denial, respect, kindness, control, money, time, and every other facet of human connections.

Friends

Solomon, one of the wisest men who ever lived, realized friends can provide more support than a sibling. He wrote, "There are 'friends' who destroy each other, but a real friend sticks closer than a brother" (Proverbs 18:24, NLT). Those who come from relatively healthy families know how to pick good friends . . . and how to avoid people who have a corrosive influence. (We'll talk more about that in chapter 10.) Those of us who come from difficult families may not have the discernment to pick good friends, but we desperately need them. In their book on the full range of relationships, Christian psychologists Les and Leslie Parrott report the results of several surveys on friendship:

> The quality that tops the list in survey after survey of what people appreciate most about their friends is loyalty. It seems nothing, but nothing, matters more than being true. Good friends keep their promises. They don't tell your secrets to other people. And they don't desert you, even when you are in trouble.
>
> The famous maxim that "a friend in need is a friend indeed" is not the entire story of loyalty, however. A friend in triumph may be even harder to find. Isn't it easier to be a savior than a cheerleader

for our friends? It takes twenty-four-karat loyalty for a friend to soar alongside us when we are flying high rather than to bring us down to earth. Loyal friends not only lend a hand when you're in need; they applaud your successes and cheer you on without envy when you prosper.[38]

What does this have to do with our family values? Quite often, great friends impart the values we didn't see and feel and incorporate when we were children. Even if our parents weren't the best role models, our friends can be ... but only if we choose the right ones and watch every move they make!

> *Show me your friends and I will show you your future.*
> —Rodney and Michelle Gage

Faith and the Bible

By now, we guess you can tell that we hold the Bible in the highest regard. It's a book with the most profound message the universe has ever heard, and it imparts that message to those who understand that reading it consistently is a magnificent treasure trove of wisdom and guidance. Many people are baffled when they begin to read the Bible. What's all that stuff about sacrifices and empires and curses? And if Jesus is full of grace and mercy, what do we do with all the "you shall"s? Great questions. From first to last, the Bible tells us about the love and power of God, our desperate need for His grace, and what it means to put Christ in the center of our lives. Yes, there are lots of commands in the Bible, often called "the law," but God knows we won't and can't fully obey Him all the time. If our relationship with God was based on our faithfulness, we'd be in big trouble. Thankfully, it's based on His faithfulness to impart His love, forgiveness, and power.

---

38   Les and Leslie Parrott, *Relationships* (Grand Rapids, MI: Zondervan, 1998), 82-83.

> *Our beliefs determine our behavior. What you believe determines how you live.*
> —Rodney Gage

How we see the Bible affects how we view not only God, ourselves, our spouse, and our kids, but also everyone and everything else in our lives. We are spiritually born again only and always by God's grace, a fact that gives us a secure foundation in this life, so we don't feel compelled to hide or control people. And His grace softens our hearts, so we love more like Jesus, loving not only the lovely but the unlovable—and everybody seems unlovable from time to time! A life lived by biblical principles and godly values allows us to love better and shine brighter to those around us, especially our family.

One of the core values that we adopted into our "Gage Family Values" is "faith," but faith in what? We have tried to help our children understand that faith is believing that God is who He says He is, and He will do what He has promised He will do, even when we don't understand Him. God sees and thinks differently than we see or think. Learning to see life from God's perspective allows us to make better choices. We love the verse in the Bible that says,

> *"My thoughts are nothing like your thoughts," says the LORD. "And my ways are far beyond anything you could imagine. For just as the heavens are higher than the earth, so my ways are higher than your ways and my thoughts higher than your thoughts."*
> —Isaiah 55:8-9 (NLT)

As we learn to put our trust in God—to walk by faith and not by sight—God begins to do something inside us. Our faith is strengthened, and our confidence begins to grow because we know God is faithful and true, and He can be trusted no matter what we face in life or temptations that my come our way. Paul assured the Christians in Philippi, "For God is working in you, giving you the desire and the power to do what pleases him" (Philippians 2:13, NLT).

TRANSFORMATION

One of the reasons why the virtue of faith is so important to us and serves as the centerpiece, anchor, and foundation to our marriage and family is because we have had a front row seat to watch miracle after miracle in our own lives. These miracles have proven God's faithfulness time and time again. We have also seen countless people in over thirty years of ministry experience radical change. People far from God. People who were spiritually lost, confused, and hopeless by the unfortunate circumstances of life. We've seen people who have had everything money could buy and achieved the highest levels of success find greater purpose through Christ. We've seen people whose lives were wrecked by the devastating choices they made find hope, forgiveness, and new beginnings through Christ. We know what we believe and why we believe it because we know that with God, all things are possible.

Let us tell you a remarkable story about a transformation. Freddie was born in a charity ward in Houston, Texas. His father was an alcoholic and a street fighter who loaded and unloaded cargo ships in the Houston ship channel, so Freddie was reared by his grandparents in one of the city's roughest ghettos. Because he was always surrounded by alcoholism, violence, and dysfunction as a child, Freddie soon followed in his father's footsteps and became involved in drugs and gang violence. By the age of sixteen, he was a leader of one of Houston's most notorious gangs and found himself in and out of juvenile detention centers during most of his teenage years.

While hanging out with friends in a roller-skating rink one night, a beautiful, petite, dark-haired girl captured Freddie's attention. He introduced himself and learned her name was Barbara. She was also an only child whose mother had been married and divorced six times. Barbara spent most of her Friday and Saturday nights at the roller-skating rink with her friends. After only a few dates, Freddie and Barbara decided to get married . . . on Barbara's fifteenth birthday. Freddie was seventeen. They both had to get their parents' written consent before they could get their marriage license.

No one was surprised when, only a few months later, Barbara filed for divorce after she saw the extent of Freddie's involvement in drugs, gangs, and crime. Barbara moved back home, and Freddie soon found himself back in jail after another arrest.

One night while Freddie was in jail, his father went to see him. Although his dad was as tough as they come, he had just attended a church service with a friend where he had a "born again" experience with Jesus Christ. After hearing a message of hope and how Christ could change a person's life, Freddie's father made a commitment in his heart that night that changed everything in his life. He told Freddie about his new conversion, and he promised to pay Freddie's jail bond for his release. There was just one catch: Freddie had to promise to attend a service at the same church his father had attended the night before. When you're stuck in jail with no prospects, who wouldn't accept that offer?!

Freddie fulfilled his promise and went to the church service the same night as his release. Upon hearing the messages of hope, forgiveness, and reconciliation with God, he responded publicly to the altar call that very night. Little did Freddie know that Barbara was also attending the same service. While he was at the altar, Barbara happened to be on the opposite side, giving *her* life to Christ too.

This may sound like a contrived story to make a dramatic point to emphasize the importance of making a major shift. And besides, just because two people claim to give their lives to Christ doesn't always result in significant changes in the way they live.

I (Rodney) can assure you that their story was more dramatic than you can imagine, and it was not at all contrived. I heard the story from their own lips and witnessed their journey of faith with my own eyes because I personally knew Barbara and Freddie as Mom and Dad.

Only God could have orchestrated the events of their early lives to have them both at the same place and same time to experience a shift that would completely change the trajectory of their lives, their marriage, and their future. Shortly after they committed their lives to Christ, God began to do a miracle work in their relationship. They eventually got back together and, as the old saying goes, the rest is history.

My parents remained together and shared over sixty-four years of marriage. My father, after his conversion, sensed God's calling on his life to go into full-time ministry. Over the course of his sixty years of ministry, God used him to win over one million people to Christ with the same message of hope, forgiveness, and reconciliation that had changed his life and marriage.

My parents are now together in their eternal home in heaven. It was their faith and commitment to teach me and my brothers the biblical principles and moral values that have helped shape who we are today.

NEVER TOO LATE

Let us encourage you to build your house on the right foundation, a foundation built on truth, stability, and an eternal promise. It takes some deep reflection and asking tough questions, but digging deep into your past and uncovering what makes you tick is vital to realigning your family and charting a course where God's values are radiant in your own family.

- What beliefs and values have shaped your life?
- What are you building your life on?
- If you have children, what beliefs and values are you teaching them?
- How have your beliefs and values influenced your marriage and family relationships?

In His famous Sermon on the Mount, Jesus addressed some controversial issues that we're still dealing with today. Jesus helped them understand two of life's most important questions: Who are you living for, and what are you living for? Are you living for yourself, or are you living for Christ? Are you living for the temporal things or the eternal things? Jesus gives a powerful word picture:

"Anyone who listens to my teaching and follows it is wise, like a person who builds a house on solid rock. Though the rain comes in torrents and the floodwaters rise and the winds beat against that house, it won't collapse because it is built on bedrock. But anyone who hears my teaching and doesn't obey it is foolish, like a person who builds a house on sand. When the rains and floods come and the winds beat against that house, it will collapse with a mighty crash." When Jesus had finished saying these things, the crowds were amazed at his teaching, for he taught with real authority—quite unlike their teachers of religious law. —Matthew 7:24-29 (NLT)

Don't build your life, marriage, and family on the sands of this culture. Don't allow the corrupt beliefs and values of this world to influence the choices you make. We've seen it firsthand if you do, and know your life will crash. We encourage you to make the shift and start today by building your life and family on the solid, unshakable truth and the promises that will stand forever.

As we stated earlier in the chapter, we both were very fortunate to have been raised in Christian homes. But just like my (Rodney's) parents, God can make changes in our lives and situation no matter what or who may have influenced us. If you have children, it is our prayer that you will find hope in what we have shared in this chapter and place your faith in God to help you make whatever shift you need to make to transform your most important relationships. Our prayer is that you will be able to say this about your children one day. It is found in 3 John 1:4 (author paraphrase), "It is the greatest joy of my life to hear that my children are consistently living their lives in the ways of truth!"

THINK ABOUT IT:

1) What are some of the strongest messages in our culture's advertising, song lyrics, fashion, and sports?
2) How do you think your family background has affected your marriage and your relationship with your children?
3) Who are some friends you admire? What are you learning from them?
4) Is the Bible inspiring or confusing to you? What can you do to learn how to understand the truths of the Bible so they transform your life?
5) How would you explain the overflow of Christ's love, forgiveness, and acceptance? What in your life stimulates your experience of these things so they spill out of you more naturally?
6) Read 2 Timothy 3:16-17. What will you allow to be the source of your beliefs and values?
7) If you have kids, read Deuteronomy 6:5-9. How will you begin to influence your children so they know what they believe and why they believe it?

DO IT:

Answer and discuss these questions as a family:

1) What does 3 John 1:4 mean to you? Commit 3 John 1:4 to memory and pray it as a blessing over your children.
2) Values in Action: No matter what messages we've absorbed from our culture, our childhood, and our friends, God can enable us to make a shift that changes everything. It's time to put into writing the changes you want to see become a reality in your marriage and family.

CHAPTER 6

WHAT GETS REWARDED GETS REPEATED

DISCOVER THE BENEFITS OF A VALUES-DRIVEN CULTURE IN YOUR HOME

Each day of our lives we make deposits in the memory banks of our children.
—Chuck Swindoll[39]

A couple of years ago, we took our daughter Ashlyn to the beach. She had come home for Spring Break from college, and she was longing to get that sun-kissed tan before she went back to school. We decided to make a day trip to one of our favorite beaches nearby. Since

---
39 Charles R. Swindoll, *The Family: A Proclamation to the World* (Colorado Springs, CO: Insight for Living, 1998).

it was Spring Break, the beaches were busier than normal. There were thousands of people on the beach that day. We finally found a spot to put our beach chairs out. We were ready to enjoy the sun and relax . . . until we overheard (actually, we couldn't help but hear!) a man not far from us yelling at his son who looked to be about eight years old. The little boy must have committed some heinous crime for his dad to react with so much anger and frustration. As we listened and watched out of the corners of our eyes, we learned that the little boy got suntan lotion in his eyes. The poor kid was obviously in pain and discomfort. Rather than quickly rushing to help his son get the lotion out of his eyes and comfort him, the father kept growling, "Quit your whining! Big boys don't cry!" We were surprised and, quite frankly, appalled at what we were witnessing, and other people noticed. It was obvious the little boy felt helpless, but the father didn't let up. He threatened his little boy, "If you don't stop crying, I'm going to get a spray bottle of vinegar from the car and squirt it in your mouth!"

    I (Rodney) was on the verge of stepping in to address the situation as were others. We were hoping the father would eventually come to his senses to show some compassion toward his son. As we continued to observe the situation, we began to wonder where the mother was. We thought we had seen her earlier, but she wasn't at the scene. Suddenly, Michelle spotted her near the shore. To our shock, she was taking "selfies" with her cell phone with a selfie stick. We didn't know if she was a fashion blogger trying to catch the "perfect pose" out on the beach, but obviously, she was totally checked out from what was going on with her son and husband. When the mom finally made her way back to her husband and little boy, she expressed her frustration and anger—at her husband. They went at it! Insults and accusations were flying. It was quite a scene. The couple quickly gathered their belongings along with their little boy and left. We, along with the small crowd of witnesses on the beach that day, were shocked at what we had witnessed. As we drove back home from the beach later that day, we couldn't get that situation out of our minds or off of our hearts.

We've often thought about that scene at the beach that day. We couldn't help but wonder what the atmosphere of their marriage and home must be like. We couldn't help but wonder what that little boy's future will be. What kind of young man will he become? Will he one day repeat the same dysfunction and destructive behavior his father displayed on the beach that day to his own children? Who knows? We pray that somehow, some way, that family will make a SHIFT for the good in their home before it's too late.

> *Every interaction, every word we speak, and every look we have on our face shapes the culture of our family.*
> —Rodney and Michelle Gage

FAMILY CULTURE

We often talk about pop culture, cultural trends in politics, and corporate culture, but every family has its own culture, too. Actually, creating a positive family culture has many parallels to a CEO establishing a healthy, productive environment in a company. An article on culture in Harvard Business Review can be applied to the atmosphere spouses create in their marriage and parents for their children. The authors assert that creating a healthy culture is one of the most important jobs of leaders:

> *For better and worse, culture and leadership are inextricably linked. Founders and influential leaders often set new cultures in motion and imprint values and assumptions that persist for decades. Over time an organization's leaders can also shape culture, through both conscious and unconscious actions (sometimes with unintended consequences). The best leaders we have observed are fully aware*

of the multiple cultures within which they are embedded, can sense when change is required, and can deftly influence the process.[40]

But a culture that builds trust and encourages creativity doesn't happen naturally. Many leaders are too disengaged, and the culture of their companies suffers. The article continues by explaining:

Unfortunately, in our experience it is far more common for leaders seeking to build high-performing organizations to be confounded by culture. Indeed, many either let it go unmanaged or relegate it to the HR function, where it becomes a secondary concern for the business. They may lay out detailed, thoughtful plans for strategy and execution, but because they don't understand culture's power and dynamics, their plans go off the rails. As someone once said, culture eats strategy for breakfast.[41]

Does this sound like any families you know? In our years of experience teaching and mentoring couples and families, we've seen many who are like the CEOs in the article—they have goals, strategies, and effort, but they "go off the rails" because they make the wrong assumptions about the unspoken but powerful forces at work in their relationships. In other words, couples need to work hard to identify, internalize, and live according to values that promote faith, honesty, love, and the other values and virtues on the lists made in the previous chapters. Perhaps the best indicator of our values is what we reward.

BECOME A GOLD DIGGER

The late Dale Carnegie was known for telling the story of how gold miners found gold. He explained that several tons of dirt had to be removed before a single ounce of gold could be found. The miners didn't go in looking for the dirt; they went in looking for the gold. That's exactly

---

40 Boris Groysberg, Jeremiah Lee, Jesse Price, and J. Yo-Jud Cheng, "The Leader's Guide to Corporate Culture," *Harvard Business Review*, January-February 2018, https://hbr.org/2018/01/the-culture-factor.

41 Boris Groysberg, et. al., "The Leader's Guide to Corporate Culture."

the way families should approach the atmosphere of their relationships. It's easy to point out the flaws, warts, blemishes, and imperfections, but to create a positive, healthy atmosphere, we need to look for the gold, sifting through the dirt, looking for the good, and discarding the bad. Like everything else, the more good qualities we look for, encourage, and reward in marriages and in children, the more good qualities we find.

THE POWER OF PRAISE

We may have very different personalities and widely varied interests, but there isn't a soul on earth that doesn't long for affirmation. That's the reward that means the most to us. It has the power to change the trajectory of a person's life, especially children who are sponges soaking up the verbal and nonverbal communication of their parents. In her book *The Power of a Woman's Words*, Sharon Jaynes recalls:

> *Many years ago I read the story of a famous artist who late in life was asked how he became an artist. He was clearly gifted as a young child, but early on things could have gone a different direction. He came home from school one afternoon and his mother was not home. He found food coloring in the kitchen, found paper, and decided to draw a picture of his sister, Sally. The carnage in the kitchen was fully complete by the time he finished his sister's portrait. Nearly an hour later when his mother came in, he saw a stunned look on her face and then she gathered him up in her arms and said, "Why, its Sally!" She told him what an incredible picture he had drawn and what a gift he had. Then, she kissed him on the forehead and told him to go get cleaned up for dinner. Years later he never failed to give credit to that amazing woman. His name was Benjamin West and his clear recognition of his Mom's affirmation should never be forgotten: "My mother's kiss made me a painter."*[42]

---

42 Sharon Jaynes, *The Power of a Woman's Words* (Eugene, OR: Harvest House Publishers, 2007), 59.

Children need to hear—and be convinced of—three consistent messages: "I love you," "I'm proud of you," and "You're really good at (a particular skill)." The first one communicates affection, the second delight, and the third that we see something special for our child's future. How often do we need to say these words? As often as they need it, which is very often, but not so much that it becomes stale and inauthentic.

I (Michelle) have talked to parents who assure us, "I give my child plenty of affirmation. I'm doing fine with that." But when I look into the eyes of the son or daughter, I don't see confidence. I see fear. Many of us give mixed messages to our spouses and children. We say, "I love you" one minute, but we scowl and condemn the next. We may think the message of love is good enough, but mixed messages are extremely confusing to any recipient. To the extent a person is wise and mature, he can handle mixed messages by confronting the conflicting voices. But the vast majority of people are vulnerable because they're too young to know better, or they're too wounded to be strong enough to discount them. Mixed messages may be the most manipulative and cause the most damage because they tap into the twin emotions of hope and fear. Those who hear these voices desperately want to hear words of love and affirmation, and each one inflames their hope to hear more ... but they are terrified they'll get harsh criticism (like the man with his boy on the beach) or icy cold isolation, which hurts just as much.

The reward of verbalized love, delight, and insight into the person's unique talents is obliterated when that message is coupled with anger, contempt, or disgust. "Yeah," you're probably saying right now, "but what about when the person fails, or worse, when she's defiant? How should I respond?" Great question.

Some of us interpret the failure of those we love as catastrophic, and we let them know it. Failure happens to all of us, but it's not the end of the world! If we can reorient our thinking and values surrounding another person's failure, it can be a big stepping stone into the future. A study by professor Kyla Haimovitz and her colleague Carol Dweck found that when parents communicate that a child's failure is debilitating, often "catastrophizing" the event and blowing it out of proportion, the message has powerfully negative effects on the child. They conclude that when a child fails, parents need to focus on what the child can learn from the experience, not the failure itself. Haimovitz encourages parents to ask their kids, "How can you use this as a jumping off point?" When parents overreact to failure, children internalize their parents' reaction and assume the parents believe failure is fatal and failure is final. What could have been a powerful learning experience turns into an event that erodes the child's confidence and limits creativity to solve problems next time.[43]

The answer, of course, isn't to be blindly positive all the time. Our kids are in a long process of learning and growing. They need to be taught, nurtured, and sometimes corrected. But when we correct them, we need to stay calm, focus on what they can learn, and communicate confidence they'll do better next time. The dad on the beach could easily have said to his son, "Hey, no problem. I'll help you get the lotion out of your eyes." And the next time they went to the beach, the dad could say before they got out of the car, "We're going to have a lot of fun today. I love being with you!"

> *Be the attitude you want to be around.*
> —Tim DeTellis[44]

FOUR STAGES

As our children grow, our parenting skills need to keep up. It would be silly to treat a high school student the way we care for a three-year-old, but sadly, some parents haven't made the transition. They still believe

---

43 Tara Haelle, "How to Teach Children that Failure Is the Secret to Success," *NPR*, May 6, 2016, https://www.npr.org/sections/health-shots/2016/05/06/476884049/how-to-teach-children-that-failure-is-the-secret-to-success.

44 Tim DeTellis, "Attitudes, Neighbors, and Motivation Plus Encouragement," *TimDeTellis*, March 23, 2023, https://timdetellis.com/2023/03/23/attitudes-neighbors-and-motivation-plus-encouragement/.

they need to tell their "almost adult" what to think, where to go, what to wear, and every other decision in their day. The goal of parenting is to launch children into adulthood with confidence, values, and the skills to succeed. To accomplish this herculean feat, we need to gradually and carefully impart more responsibility to our children. And at every age, even long after they've left and begun their own families, they need to keep hearing the three foundational messages: "I love you," "I'm proud of you," and "You're good at this or that."

We've identified four stages of parenting, and in each of them, we need to reward the right things, behaviors, and values.

Stage 1: Birth to five years old—Tenderhearted Supervisor

In the early years, children haven't internalized the ability to make wise decisions—not by a long shot! Our role in this stage is to lovingly supervise them and reinforce good behavior. Solomon reminds us, "A refusal to correct is a refusal to love; love your children by disciplining them" (Proverbs 13:24, MSG). Discipline is not something we do to our children; it is something we do for our children. Discipline isn't only correcting children who misbehave; it's also instructing, guiding, and encouraging right choices.

In this stage, we **reward obedience.**

Stage 2: Six to twelve years old—Fitness Trainer

In this stage, children are growing physically, emotionally, intellectually, and relationally. It's our role to give them the resources they need to stimulate each of these areas of growth. In Stage 1, we gave instructions; here, we ask questions to help them think and find the best solution. Gradually, we see them grow in their confidence and abilities.

In this stage, we **reward good choices.**

Stage 3: Thirteen to eighteen years old—Coach

If we give children plenty of instructions when they're little and lots of resources as they grow, they'll have much of what they need when they get to this stage. Our role here is to coach them, to affirm good decisions, help them learn from failure, and stimulate their creativity. We stop making so many decisions for them, and we expect them (require them) to make more of their own.

In this stage, we ***reward growing responsibility and independence.***

Stage 4: Over eighteen years old—Consultant and Friend

When our children leave home for work, the military, or college, we launch them with the hope they'll apply all they've learned since they were babies. But we're not finished. We take on a new role of consultant and, sooner or later, peer and friend. If they know we respect them, they'll want our input. When that happens, we need to avoid regressing to our role as Fitness Trainer or Coach. We give input but with the freedom for our grown son or daughter to make the decision. Here, we're letting go of control and trusting that our child will have the wisdom to find success and handle difficulties with calm confidence. We begin to see the legacy of our love and values passed down to their children.

In this stage, we ***reward values being imparted to the next generation.***

> *The goal of parenting is to launch children into adulthood with the confidence, values, and skills to succeed.*
> —Rodney and Michelle Gage

LIFE IS AN ECHO

Whatever we reward will be repeated. It's a principle of human nature and of the kingdom of God. It's important, though, to look beneath actions to notice, name, and nurture the qualities, values, and characteristics we see. We look under the hood to see the engine of each person's motivation—when they succeed and when they fail. The goal is to focus on affirming and recognizing positive qualities, choices, and behaviors rather than focusing on the negative. In other words, be a good finder. Why is this so important? Because the way we see people is the way we treat them, and the way we treat them is the way they often become.

I (Rodney) love the story the late Zig Ziglar tells in his famous book *See You at the Top*: [There was a] little boy who, in a fit of anger, shouted to his mother that he hated her. Then, perhaps fearing punishment, he ran out of the house to the hillside and shouted into the valley, "I hate you, I hate you, I hate you." Back from the valley came the echo, "I hate you, I hate you, I hate you." Somewhat startled, the little boy ran back into the house and told his mother there was a mean little boy in the valley saying he hated him. His mother took him back to the hillside and told him to shout, "I love you, I love you." The little boy did as his mother said, and this time, he discovered there was a nice little boy in the valley saying, "I love you, I love you."

Ziglar shares a vital lesson that comes straight from the Bible. The Bible teaches us in Galatians 6:7 that we reap what we sow. If we sow consistency in our love and affirmations, our spouses and children will reap those traits. Ziglar concludes the story with the lesson: "Life is an echo. What you send out—comes back. What you sow—you reap. What you give—you get. What you see in others—exists in you."[45] Let's commit to being good finders, to look for the gold, not the dirt, and to celebrate and reward the good. You will find that what you reward gets repeated.

A friend told us that when his daughter was in high school, she excelled in technology and entered a district contest. She didn't win, but our friend didn't focus on her failure, didn't berate the judge for being unfair, and didn't say anything about the other contestants. He hugged his daughter and told her, "I'm so proud of you! Through all of your training for this contest, you showed dedication, and you really enjoyed learning. And I saw you encourage the girl sitting next to you. I couldn't be happier right now. There's no telling where this skill may take you."

Another dad had a beautiful daughter. He saw how other attractive high school girls were obsessed with their appearance and fashion. The parents of the other girls reinforced this obsession, but this father

---

45 Zig Ziglar, *See You at the Top*, 25th anniversary ed. (Gretna, LA: Pelican Publishing, 2000)

wanted to give his daughter a different perspective. He told her, "You're very attractive. Everybody can see that. But there's something far more important than appearance—it's character. I appreciate your heart for God, the way you treat people, and the fact that you relate to everybody, from little children to old people. You bring joy to every person you meet. Make sure you never lose that. It's priceless." She didn't forget. Today, she has two children of her own, and she's having similar talks with them.

A FRESH START

You may be reading this and thinking, *Rodney and Michelle, you don't get it. You have no idea how badly I've messed up. I've hurt people, and the way I've treated them has caused a lot of damage. I'm not sure it can ever be any different.*

Here's the good news: Today is a new day—you can have a fresh start. It's never too late to impart love, honesty, faith and other values to the people who mean so much to you. But progress isn't cheap. It requires us to let God use His scalpel to open our hearts so He can do surgery on the damaged parts of our lives. When we experience God's healing, we'll be different, and we can treat our families with kindness instead of harshness, love instead of intimidation, and respect instead of fostering fear.

Lauri was raised by a demanding mother who was never satisfied with Lauri's performance. Her mother smiled at people outside the home, but inside the walls, she was a bear! Lauri's father knew better than to poke the bear, so he became passive, a non-factor in the house. But his lack of attention, affection, and protection left Lauri and her brother vulnerable to her mom's condemnation. To no one's surprise, when Lauri grew up and got married, she treated her two girls the way her mother had treated her. She hated it, but her mother's attitude and actions were deeply ingrained in her. She had never seen another way to relate to children.

When her older daughter was ten and the younger was eight years old, Lauri realized how much she was hurting them, so she got an appointment with a counselor. She had always assured herself that she was a good mother and never needed anyone's help—especially a counselor's. Now, though, she realized she simply couldn't deny the reality that she was harming the souls of her daughters. In counseling, she poured out her fear and anger that had been pent up for decades. It was exhausting, and she wanted to quit a thousand times, but she kept going. Gradually, the wounds of the past were healed, and Lauri experienced more of God's grace than she ever imagined possible. As she grew strong and whole, she apologized to her daughters. She invited them to be completely honest about the pain she had caused them, and together, they healed past hurts, expressed and experienced love, and created a very different atmosphere in their home.

No matter where you've come from and what you'd done, it's never too late to take God's hand and start over. One of the most encouraging passages in the Bible is a psalm that shows that God never gives up on us. Asaph was deeply disappointed with the way his life was working out, and he wrote:

Then I realized that my heart was bitter,
and I was all torn up inside.
I was so foolish and ignorant—
I must have seemed like a senseless animal to you.
Yet I still belong to you;
you hold my right hand.
You guide me with your counsel,
leading me to a glorious destiny. —Psalm 73:21-24 (NLT)

You may be at the point of being so angry and frustrated that you feel like "a senseless failure." But even if you're not there, you probably know someone who is. God's assurance is that we're never out of reach. He still holds our hands, guides us in a better path, and takes us to a place where we experience far more of His love, forgiveness, and power. You can start over.

The goal as parents isn't to ensure our kids get a good education, land a good job, find a spouse, and give us grandchildren. The goal is that our kids grow wise and strong, living values that are far higher and far deeper than anything the world thinks is important. When they internalize God's values, they'll have an impact on their generation no matter what their career path looks like, and they'll instill these values in their children, leaving a legacy for the generations to come. This can only happen if we reward the right things.

We turn again to Solomon, who gives us sage advice: "Dedicate your children to God and point them in the way that they should go, and the values they've learned from you will be with them for life" (Proverbs 22:6, TPT). The way we relate to our spouse and kids is pointing them in a certain direction. Stop the drift, make the shift . . . to change the atmosphere and culture of our homes. We can change. We become what we're committed to!

THINK ABOUT IT:
1) What are some things that might have been the underlying cause of the anger and intimidation of the man on the beach? Do you have any compassion for him? Why or why not?
2) How would you describe the culture of your family? What would a perceptive person from the outside say about it?
3) Describe the power of affirmation.
4) What attitudes and behaviors were rewarded when you were a child?
5) In which of the roles in the four stages of parenting do you feel most comfortable? Which one feels most uncomfortable? Explain your answers.
6) Why is it so important to "look under the hood" and notice, name, and nurture the values you see in your spouse and children?

7) On a scale of 0 (none) to 10 (off the charts), how much hope do you have that you can learn to reward the right things in the members of your family? What are you doing well now? What needs to change?

DO IT:
Answer and discuss these questions as a family:
1) Have a conversation with your spouse about the changing stages of parenting your kids.
2) When you've identified your current role, take two steps to fulfill your role in each child's stage.

STEP 3

IDENTIFY YOUR GPS

A SHIFT IN MOTIVATION

CHAPTER 7

ENVISION THE FUTURE

GPS: CLARIFY YOUR GOALS

We are what we repeatedly do. Excellence, then, is not an act, but a habit.
—Aristotle

Did we lose you when you read the title of this chapter? The truth is that some people love to set goals, but others despise them. Is that too strong a word? Not for those whose stomachs churn whenever anyone talks about nailing down specific goals. For those who have experienced failed attempts in the past when it comes to goals, they'd rather have a root canal with no anesthesia than set more goals. What causes such widely varied responses to the idea of establishing goals? There are several reasons.

First, some people are temperamentally wired to be concrete in their thinking. They don't like abstractions. They only feel comfortable when a plan is carefully spelled out. These are the people who get frustrated when they're invited by a friend to do something fun, but the friend either won't agree on an activity or changes plans without any notice. This is the employee who always asks for a crystal-clear goal, plan, and deadline. He wants to know exactly what's expected and what it will take to succeed. This is the spouse who makes lists, and maybe lists of lists, and writes out what she's going to take on a vacation, has an iron-clad budget, and has every item of clothing neatly folded or hung. Without a plan, these people feel out of control.

But there are people on the opposite end of the spectrum—and people in the first group are often married to them! To them, rules, plans, schedules, deadlines, and clear expectations make them feel trapped. They value freedom of expression and feel comfortable with open-ended concepts. A deadline makes them tense, unless they completely ignore it, which is the way many of them handle it. This is the friend who doesn't care what they do with you as long as you're together. This is the employee who may be wonderfully talented but drives managers and colleagues crazy by getting off track in meetings and being late with work. This is the spouse who spends without a budget, loves to make spontaneous decisions, and lives for excitement and freedom.

Into this mix, we throw our kids, who may be just as different from one another as their parents.

In the third step of our 5-Step Plan, we're going to look at the guidance system of a family, the GPS: goals, passions, and how we can respond to struggles in ways that help us grow stronger. But first, let me (Rodney) tell you about an experience our family had setting goals.

Michelle and I came to our marriage from very different backgrounds. I'm the youngest of four boys, and she's the oldest of four girls. My family was very competitive and risk-taking. Her family was very affectionate and conservative. She's a typical "oldest child" who is conscientious and very responsible. I roll the dice and play things more loosely—you middle or youngest born know what I mean. We may have been very different, but we were partners in a dumb decision early in our marriage. When we got married, both of us had cars that were paid for. No car payment is what most families long for, right? We wanted a sports car. Michelle drove an old Chevy Camaro (canary yellow) that was falling apart, and I had a Jeep. We decided to sell Michelle's car and trade my Jeep Cherokee for a tiny, two-door Mitsubishi Eclipse Turbo. And we went into debt to get it. It didn't take us long to realize it was a really dumb decision. Our goal of looking cool wasn't as important as the goal of being financially responsible. The problem is that we hadn't yet identified our goals. Chances are, we're not alone.

Let's be real. Virtually every company, large and small, every church, and every other organization invests time, energy, research, and dollars to set goals that give both direction and motivation to everyone involved. But we've noticed that couples and families seldom even have goal-setting on their radar. These relationships are the most important ones we have had, have now, and will ever have. It's important to have clear goals that enable us to bring our mission and vision forward with tangible, specific, and measurable steps. We like to call them F.A.I.T.H. goals to live by.

Focused: They must be specific.

Attainable: They must be realistic and practical.

Individual: They must be your goals, not someone else's.

Trackable: You must be able to measure progress.

Heartfelt: Your goals should motivate you and ignite your passion.

SETTING TARGETS

In his book *Your Best Year Ever*, Michael Hyatt identifies ten specific areas in which to set goals.[46] Zig Ziglar's "Wheel of Life" focuses on seven

---

46 Michael Hyatt, *Your Best Year Ever*.

areas.[47] However, we propose five targeted areas specific to setting goals for your marriage and family. We envision these areas as limbs on a tree.

The house where we lived as our kids grew up had an oak tree in the backyard—experts told us it was nearly two hundred years old. It had been struck by lightning, survived multiple hurricanes, and endured droughts. It was massive. An old swing dangled from a rope attached to one of the limbs, and our kids loved to swing on it. We pushed them so high that they'd swing higher than our neighbor's fence. One day, I asked an arborist if it was dangerous for us to be swinging our kids from that particular branch. He looked at me and said, "Sir, you could hang a Volkswagen Bug from that tree limb, and it wouldn't faze it."

When a tree is healthy, it grows organically and bears fruit. In the same way, a strong, healthy family that's rooted in the healthy soil of right beliefs will grow as strong as a mighty oak and withstand the storms and obstacles that inevitably come. The mission, vision, and values are the nutrients the roots absorb and bring to all five "limbs" or components to life:

The Family Goal Tree is a perfect metaphor for a life of growth and strength. Our values are the roots that sink deep in fertile soil to nourish our dreams. The mission and vision statements your family creates serve as the ground, the foundation, the soil your tree will use to grow. Each limb of the tree clarifies and solidifies choices.

---

47 Tom Zigler, "The Wheel of Life," *Ziglar*, https://www.ziglar.com/articles/the-wheel-of-life/.

And as these limbs grow, the whole tree becomes fortified. Like the tree, our families need to be focused on five limbs of growth.

Spiritual

Growing spiritually is not a destination, it's a journey. We are as close to God as we choose to be. Every day, we should strive to sow spiritual seeds of growth so that we can develop deeper roots of our faith. How? Through daily Bible reading, memorizing scriptures, prayer, attending church, serving, sharing our faith with nonbelievers, and doing life with others followers of Christ. We get out of our spiritual life what we put into it. Our daily routines and habits foster spiritual growth and success. Sowing these seeds has a compound effect on our lives, and consistently doing so keeps the soil of our hearts fertile and soft. The by-product is spiritual confidence. On a scale of one (bad) to ten (great) where would you and each member of your family rate your current relationships with God? What are two or three goals you can put into action to move the needle on your family's spiritual growth?

Relational

As James 4:8 teaches us, when we come close to God, He will come close to us. Our God is a relational God. He made us so He could love us and have a relationship with us. Therefore, the stronger we are spiritually in our relationship with God, the stronger our relationships will be with each other. It's important that we become students of each other's needs, personalities, passions, etc., and nurture those in a way that produces trust, honor, love, and support. When we sow into our relationships we reap the fruit of those relationships. Again, it keeps the soil of our hearts fertile, soft, and open toward each other. Using the same scale as above, from one to ten, how would you rate your current relationships with your spouse and children? What are two or three goals you can put into actions to deepen and strengthen your relationships with each other?

Financial

The Bible teaches us in Matthew 6:21 "Your heart will always pursue what you value as your treasure" (TPT). If making money and having financial security are what you value as your treasures, then these things usually takes priority over everything else. There is nothing wrong with earning and having money. Nor is there anything wrong with financial security. The purpose of setting financial goals is to be prepared for the future. The question is, Who, where, and what are we putting our trust in? Growing financially is about living in freedom rather than bondage. God wants to be first in every area of our lives, including our finances. A good goal to strive for when it comes to growing financially is to give 10 percent, save 10 percent, and live on 80 percent of what you earn. Alignment with God's plan puts us under the umbrella of His provision and protection, which is the ultimate form of security. As with the previous limbs, when we sow into eternal things, our hearts remain fertile toward the things that matter most. Using the scale of one to ten, how would you rate your current financial state as a family? What are two or three goals you can set as a couple or as a family to help set up your lives for financial success?

Intellectual

The difference between where you are and where you desire to be is what you know. We should always be sowing seeds into our own personal growth. Whether through reading books or articles, listen to podcasts, attending seminars or webinars, getting an additional academic degree, or pursuing more job training, it is important that we keep growing and stretching to reach our God-given potential. We not only need this personally and professionally, but our kids also need to be challenged and inspired to do their best and to become people of excellence. On a scale of one to ten, how would you rate your satisfaction with what you know today? Using the same scale, how motivated are you and your family to pursue new knowledge? What are two or three goals you could put into action that will help you grow from where you are to where you desire to be personally, professionally, and academically?

Physical

Why is this so important? Because we want to be at our best for the people we love the most and to fully enjoy this one and only life we have. Giving our best means having the strength, stamina, and energy to run the race God has called us to run. We set goals for growing physically in our lives to give God and each other our very best as stewards of our bodies. Physical activities are a wonderful way for our families to spend time together, grow closer, and honor God by honoring our bodies. On a scale of one to ten, how would you rate your physical fitness? What are two or three goals you could put into action as an individual, couple, or family that will move the needle to growing stronger and healthier?

In each area of growth, we encounter obstacles—reasons to quit or give less than our best. Don't be surprised when you run up against roadblocks and delays. Every good endeavor requires tenacity. Author Chuck Swindoll, says, "The longer I live the more convinced I become that life is 10 percent what happens to you and 90 percent how we respond to it."[48] We can't control what happens to us, but we can choose how we respond to difficult situations and circumstances. In each of these five areas, pursue excellence and never stop growing. Optimism is essential—not blind optimism, but open-eyed confidence that God will give you the wisdom to walk through open doors. The immediate problems can overwhelm us, so we need to keep our eyes on our hopes that God will do magnificent things in us, for us, and through us five to ten years down the road. We (Rodney and Michelle) have a sign in our kitchen that a friend gifted to us that reminds us of our Family Goal Tree and the five

---

[48] Charles R. Swindoll, *Life Is 10% What Happens to You and 90% How You React: Cultivating Inner Strength and Embracing Hope When Life Is Not What You Expected* (Nashville: Nelson Books, an imprint of Thomas Nelson, 2023).

branches of growth. It says, "We all grow in different directions but our roots remain the same."

> *The best way to lead your kids is to let them see you grow.*
> —Rodney and Michelle Gage

FOCUSED AND FLEXIBLE

Top executives in business know the importance of setting clear goals. The life of the company depends on thorough planning, clear delegation, and excellence in implementation. However, one of the chief complaints of employees is that their team leader fails to provide this kind of input. When each person has to guess what's important and when something needs to be accomplished, frustration and anger inevitably result, along with lower productivity.

Are families any different? Yes and no. The scope of goal-setting for a couple or a family isn't as comprehensive as a business plan, but it's just as important. Why don't most families have goals? Pain. That's the reason. It's too painful. Those who are naturally bent toward setting goals feel the pain of trying to get everyone in the family on board, and after multiple attempts, the pain seems greater than the benefits. Those on the other end feel misunderstood, disrespected, and even oppressed when someone in the family tries to make them set and accomplish specific goals. That's their version of too much pain and too few benefits.

Does the Bible give us an answer to this dilemma? Yes, lots of answers, and a wonderful balance between the two extremes. The book of Proverbs contains many insights about setting goals. For instance, Solomon explains, "Wise people think before they act; fools don't—and even brag about their foolishness" (Proverbs 13:16, NLT), and he reminds us that our plans aren't the only game in town: "You can make many plans, but the Lord's purpose will prevail" (Proverbs 19:21, NLT).

In fact, in the Lord's Prayer, we see this blend and balance. Jesus taught us to pray, "Our Father in heaven, may your name be kept holy. May your Kingdom come soon. May your will be done on earth, as it is in heaven" (Matthew 6:9-10, NLT). This means it should be our clear goal to plan and prioritize everything in our lives to bring God's kingdom of kindness, love, forgiveness, truth, and righteousness to our homes, schools, neighborhoods, and jobs. But life often throws us curve balls. In the surprises that happen, God is still working, accomplishing His will through the unexpected blessings and heartaches. We need to be both focused and flexible.

OVERCOMING THE PAIN

Let's face it: All of us feel disappointed or frustrated by people who see goals differently than we do. We've tried to set and live by clear goals ... or avoid what we perceive as the straightjacket of goals ... but some people we care about don't see things the way we do. Usually, the disagreement is just a mild rash, but sometimes, it's the flu! Far too many of us have become defensive, expecting the conflict and trying to manipulate and manage our way around the problem.

There's a better way.

We need to focus on the benefits the other person will receive by setting and achieving goals. That's right, *the other person*. If we only think (or primarily think) about what we want, we'll keep butting heads. But if we enter the other person's world, discover what matters to him, and then craft the process and the plans so he sees the benefit, everybody wins. It's not that hard. The loose, creative, fly-by-the-seat-of-your-pants person can realize his wife needs more structure, clear expectations, and at least a ballpark goal for the most important elements in her life. If they both focus on the benefits of compromise and moving toward each other, they will tap into each person's heartfelt motivation. Instead of pain, setting goals together can become rewarding, and eventually, both can be thrilled that they're working together toward their shared objectives.

When I (Rodney) was in high school, I had a serious motorcycle accident while attempting to race motocross. At the time, I didn't realize the impact it would have on my neck, ultimately causing me to suffer from three herniated discs. Eventually, I developed chronic neck and back pain, and I found myself in the chiropractor's office quite often. My pain usually was in the upper-middle part of my back, between my shoulder blades; however, the first time the doctor gave me an adjustment, he worked on my neck. I argued that my pain was between my shoulder blades, but he explained that I was experiencing "referred pain." I was feeling pain in one area that was actually being caused in another area. I was out of alignment. He made an adjustment to my neck which relieved the pain and discomfort in the upper-middle part of my back.

We (Rodney and Michelle) meet a lot of people who feel pain and discomfort in different areas of their lives—struggling marriage, poor health, stress at work or in other relationships, financial problems, etc. One of the things we've learned is that the pain they feel may not actually be the real problem. The pain can be a symptom of another cause. Most of the time, the pain is due to a misalignment with their goals and purpose, and they need to make necessary adjustments to get back in proper alignment with one another so that they are working together to achieve their goals. So how do you do that?

A GOAL-SETTING STRATEGY

Let us offer a strategy to help you and your family focus on the benefits of planning and set goals that motivate you to accomplish them.

Dream

Don't start with a calendar and a budget sheet. Instead, start with plenty of time to think, dream, and imagine what your family can be. This is second nature to the free-thinking people in the family, but the more structured ones need it just as much. Don't criticize anyone's ideas. Just talk. Let your mind imagine what your relationships might become, fun times, meaningful ways you can serve together, and what it will mean to instill God's values into your children. Some will want to rush through this. Don't do it! Spend several unhurried stretches of time together to let the ideas marinate. You may want to do this first as a couple, but if your children can participate, include them in a second phase of dreaming big dreams. You may have already done some big dreaming when you wrote your family mission and vision.

Set Major Goals

If you've dreamed together and found common ground, it'll be easy to write down the goals that have surfaced for your marriage and your family. Some people prefer to have one or two major goals in each of the five areas of spiritual, physical, intellectual, financial, and relational limbs of the Goal Growth Tree. These can be as specific as having dinner three times a week with the whole family, having a weekly date night, saving a particular amount of money, exercising a certain amount of time and days each week, and other specific, attainable goals.

Make sure everyone is involved. If they aren't allowed to give their input, they probably won't own the goals. You'll need to help the younger children set their goals, but as they get older and have more abilities in thinking and decision-making, encourage them to come up with their own goals.

Some of the goals for kids won't be on the lists they make. They probably won't be thrilled to be asked to make their beds, put up their clothes, and do some household chores, but these will build character. Sweeten the deal by rewarding them with something they like and enjoy if they reach these goals each week. But make sure they also have goals they're excited about pursuing and reaching.

Establish Priorities

Unfortunately, most people's lives aren't defined by what's important but by what's urgent. The tyranny of the urgent gets us out of alignment with the things that matter most in our marriages and family relationships. Author John Maxwell, in his book *Intentional Living*, writes, "Everything worthwhile is uphill."[49] The reason why worthwhile things are uphill is simply that they don't come easily. We have to fight for them. We have to decide what's important to us and fight to protect those things that will bring us purpose, joy, and fulfillment.

Many of us are already stressed by all the things we're trying to do, so perhaps the first priority is to weed out some things from the schedule. Our closets can be cluttered, but so can our schedules! We recommend you look at your major goals and put them in three categories: now, soon, and later. You may have some huge concerns that need to be addressed right away. Focus on those for a while and get them resolved, and then move to the next things on the list. You may need to negotiate what's in each category, and again, relax, focus on what motivates the other people in your family, be flexible, and compromise.

Of course, make goals age-appropriate for your children. Picking up toys every night before bed might be one of the only goals of a toddler, but as children grow, you can help them set goals that will build character as well as bring fulfillment and joy to their lives.

Here are some things we did that can serve as suggestions for you and your family:

1) Plan a weekly family fun night. Keep this sacred.
2) Have dinner together at least three to four nights a week.
3) Have consistent date nights for Mom and Dad ONLY. Keep this sacred.
4) Pray together at meal time and over our children each night.
5) Serve at church or in the community.

---

49 John C. Maxwell, *No Limits: Blow the Cap Off Your Capacity* (New York, NY: Center Street, 2017), 134.

6) Give financially to God through the tithe (10 percent of our weekly earnings).

Post Your Goals

In *Your Best Year Ever*, author Michael Hyatt writes, "What gets scheduled gets done."[50] It's important to keep your family's goals in front of you, especially on your calendar. Get everyone involved to post your goals on the refrigerator, make a screensaver or put sticky notes on your vision board where everyone can see them. If a goal is reached by increments, like saving money for a bike or a vacation, you can create a "thermometer" and mark each step of progress. At one point, we had a giant plastic Coke bottle that we used to put our spare change in. It was our way of saving up for our summer vacations. The day before we left to go on vacation, we took all the coins we had saved in the bottle to the coin machine at the grocery store to count it and convert it to cash. Before we had the total, we let each person guess the amount. We used the money to do fun things on vacation. The kids loved it, and it served as motivation to give and save.

Start Small

It's really important to have enough wins that everyone in the family stays motivated. Small successes are more easily achieved and keep the ball rolling toward bigger goals. We recommend having some goals that can be accomplished in a day (daily goals like making the bed or putting dishes away) or at most a week (weekly goals like mowing the lawn, setting the week's agenda, meal planning for the week). When people have a sense of accomplishment, they'll be encouraged and strive even more.

Take Inventory

Goals and plans that aren't regularly evaluated are easily forgotten. Most of us have had that experience. We started an endeavor with big

---

50   Michael Hyatt, *Your Best Year Ever*.

dreams and clear plans, but over months and years, the initial vision faded to black. Don't let that happen! Create a "time block" or call a "family huddle" at the beginning of each month to reflect, review, and evaluate your progress. Are you in proper alignment with the things you say are important? If not, make an adjustment so that your life is in proper alignment with your goals, purpose, and priorities. Don't be afraid to shift your goals and priorities to keep each person motivated. In these conversations, don't focus on what wasn't accomplished and goals that weren't met. First, camp out in the successes and spend most of your time there. Always come back to the benefits of each goal for each person to keep them motivated. Duty motivates some people, but benefits motivate everybody.

Celebrate All Along the Way

Don't wait until a big goal is reached to celebrate. Make a big deal of the steps your family is taking on the road to completion and growth. We've already looked at the power of affirmation; look for ways to tell people, "You're making progress! Way to go!"

> *The five most important words we can ever say are "You did a great job!"*
> —Rodney and Michelle Gage.

Make goal-setting fun. If setting goals and pursuing them is a grind, the process is doomed from the beginning. Whatever it takes, make it fun. Dream, laugh, and encourage big dreams and small steps forward.

Does all this seem like a mountain too big to climb? We hope not. Yes, it takes time to think, pray, dream, and plan, but it's well worth it. Setting family goals and creating an atmosphere of enthusiasm to reach them is one of the biggest shifts a family can make. Great families don't happen by chance, and they aren't created by magic. It's all about living with greater intention. Setting inspiring goals and making progress toward them stops the drift and motivates the shift.

THINK ABOUT IT:

1) On the spectrum of structured to free-wheeling, where does each person in your family fall? Have the differences created tension in the past around goals and steps to reach them? If so, give some examples.

2) What saps your energy and enthusiasm about setting goals at work, in school, or in your family? What excites you?

3) Pick one person in your family who is different from you in how you set goals. Enter that person's world and describe what motivates him or her. What benefits of setting goals and reaching them rev that person's engine?

4) Why is starting out with imagination so important?

5) What are some specific, age-appropriate goals for your children?

6) Describe how you plan to go through a process of crafting, pursuing, and staying on track with your family's goals. What difference will it make for you and for them?

DO IT:

Answer and discuss these questions as a family:

1) Use the worksheet on the next page to craft your goals.

2) In the next few days, schedule a time for you to talk with your spouse and imagine what God wants to do in and through your family. Then, when you have identified some hopes and dreams, carve out time in the next week to go through the worksheet. The goal isn't to complete it but to let it represent your family's hearts' desires to honor God and create an environment in which each person soars!

FAMILY GOALS

Review
What is the mission of your family?

_____
_____
_____
_____

What are your family's values?

_____
_____
_____
_____

What is your vision of the impact God will have through your family?

_____
_____
_____
_____

Long-term
In each of these areas, write all the goals you want to achieve in the next one to three years. (You'll need additional paper.)
- Physical

_____
_____

- Spiritual

_____
_____

- Intellectual

_____
_____

- Financial

_____
_____

- Relational

_____
_____

Focused and Soon

Now, identify one or two specific, measurable goals you want to focus on in each area:

- Physical

_____
_____

- Spiritual

_____
_____

- Intellectual

_____
_____

- Financial

- Relational

What will be the benefits of reaching these goals?

When will you take the first step for each of them?

CHAPTER 8

DOING WHAT COMES NATURALLY

GPS: PURSUE YOUR PASSIONS

Your purpose guides you, but your passion drives you.
—Michelle Gage

If we'll let them, our biggest struggles can shift our priorities and refine our direction. When our daughter Ashlyn was thirteen, she developed chronic hives that wouldn't go away. The dermatologist gave her strong medicine, but it didn't help much. We tried other doctors and did whatever they recommended. We took out all of our carpets to eliminate dust, and we became detectives to expose any kind of irritant to her skin. The medicines had side effects of drowsiness, making it difficult for her to concentrate in school. The itching, pain, and sleepiness made life very hard for our little girl. Finally, after a long year, the hives began to subside. Through all of this, Ashlyn kept a positive attitude. In fact, she went out for the tennis team when she was a freshman and made varsity. By the time she graduated, she was the top player on the team, and she won academic honors. Her experiences of suffering with the hives gave her compassion for others who struggle with health problems, so much so that at the time of our writing this book, she is currently pursuing a degree in medicine with a goal to get her master's and become a physician's assistant. She's a wonderful example of someone whose passion came out of persevering through pain and problems.

Our deepest desires can consume every waking moment, thrill us, and energize us to accomplish great things, or they can terrify us and cause us to wilt under the pressure of facing success or failure. In other words, our passions can rule us, inspire us, or shackle us.

We've explored some deep questions in this book so far: What are we living for? Who are we becoming? Why do we get up each day? What are the values that shape our lives and our families? And how do we get where we want to go? We've learned that having mission and vision statements and creating values help us clarify and answer these important questions. Now, we can look closer at the engine of our lives: our passion to fulfill our highest aspirations.

Passion isn't just emotion. It's more than that. Having passion is your drive, determination, expectation, and joy in taking each step forward towards something (goal, dream, place in life, etc.). Far too many of us have ambitions that are too small, so our passions aren't ignited. And far too often, our ambitions are disconnected from our relationship with God.

He wants our relationships with one another to mirror the same spirit He gives each of us individually. In the last chapter, we looked at the importance of setting goals. The five life area goals go far beyond superficial pursuits of wealth, beauty, pleasure, and power. If God gives us those things, we can use them for bigger purposes. Our greatest ambition should be to know God and make Him known through our successes and in our marriage and family relationships.

> *A great leader's courage to fulfill his vision
> comes from passion, not position.*
> —John C. Maxwell[51]

THE TRUTH ABOUT AMBITION

We often think of "ambition" as a negative term because we assume it necessarily implies selfishness. It often does, but not always—the rightness or wrongness of ambition is in its aim. In Paul's second letter to the Christians in Corinth, he explains that we need to have an eternal perspective and realize this life isn't all there is. Someday, as believers we'll be with Christ face-to-face. Living with Him is our true, eternal home. This assurance gives us hope and clarifies our goals each and every day. He wrote, "Therefore, we also have as our ambition, whether at home or absent, to be pleasing to Him" (2 Corinthians 5:9, NASB). Ambition to please God is good, right, and noble.

Does it please God to have relationships with our spouse and children that affirm them, protect them, and inspire them to become strong, healthy, creative people? Of course it does! Does it please God to enjoy one another and resolve disagreements? You bet. Does it please Him when we give generously and work together to serve people who are disadvantaged? Yes. These are just a taste of the many ambitions that we want to encourage and model as spouses and parents.

The most important commandment in the Bible is called the Great Commandment. We love how *The Message* translation describes it: "Love the Lord God with all your passion and prayer and intelligence and energy" (Mark 12:30, MSG).

God is a passionate God—He also feels things deeply. Since we are created in His image, God has created us to be passionate people. He not only wants us to love Him passionately, but He also wants us to live our

---

51 John C. Maxwell, *The 21 Indispensable Qualities of a Leader: Becoming the Person Others Will Want to Follow* (Nashville, TN: Thomas Nelson, 2007), 89.

lives full of passion—fully alive. In Romans 12:11, Paul writes (emphasis added), "Never be lacking in zeal, but *keep* your spiritual fervor, serving the Lord." Notice the emphasis on the word "keep." That tells us that passion is something we can lose if we're not careful. We have to work at keeping our passion fully alive because if we don't, we can lose our passion for the Lord and our passion for life.

As all of us know, life itself can beat the passion right out of us. Our schedules may be full, but our lives can be empty.

When our lives become overcrowded, how do we restore and rejuvenate our passion?

One of our favorite stories in the Bible is about some men who desperately wanted to see their paralyzed friend healed. Luke records the event:

> *Some men came carrying a paralyzed man on a mat and tried to take him into the house to lay him before Jesus. When they could not find a way to do this because of the crowd, they went up on the roof and lowered him on his mat through the tiles into the middle of the crowd, right in front of Jesus. When Jesus saw their faith, he said, "Friend, your sins are forgiven. . . . But I want you to know that the Son of Man has authority on earth to forgive sins." So he said to the paralyzed man, "I tell you, get up, take your mat and go home." Immediately he stood up in front of them, took what he had been lying on and went home praising God. Everyone was amazed and gave praise to God. They were filled with awe and said, "We have seen remarkable things today." —Luke 5:18-26*

We love this story because of the determination and persistence of these men to get their friend to Jesus. You might wonder what this story has to do with restoring our passion for our marriage and family. These men faced what we all face . . . problems and setbacks: "They could not find a way to do this because of the crowd" (verse 19).

A crowded life will rob us of our joy and passion. The worst thing about a crowded life is that it keeps us from being close to Christ. We know because we've experienced it. I heard someone say that the word B.U.S.Y. stands for Being Under Satan's Yoke. The enemy of our souls wants to get us so busy that we don't have the time or the energy for the people who matter most in our lives, let alone God. Let us share with you four things we can do to keep our passion alive.

Do Something Drastic

In our book *ReThink Life*,[52] I (Rodney) tell the story of when, years ago, I was challenged by several staff members to go skydiving. I can't stand heights, so jumping out of an airplane seemed outright crazy! While I consider myself a risk-taker, taking that kind of risk was something I definitely never thought I would do. However, I've also learned to never say *never*. Reluctantly, I agreed to this insanity. Jubilantly, my friends arranged all the details.

Needless to say, I didn't sleep much the night before our jump. Tossing and turning all night, I wondered if it would be my last night to live. Morning came too soon. Bright and early, my eager friends arrived to drive me to the private airport.

We sat through a short orientation. We watched a video about skydiving, received directions, and were warned about the risks involved. After signing our lives away, we were escorted into a dressing room to put on our gear. After meeting our instructor and receiving a few tips, my friends and I were rushed to the airplane for our jump. I guess the instructor's reasoning for being so hurried was to avoid having anyone (like me) chicken out.

I'll never forget taxiing down the runway, taking off, and having reality hit me that I was actually getting ready to jump out of an airplane at thirteen thousand feet and a speed of over 100 mph . . . strapped to a guy I didn't know. I was freaking out!

---

52   Rodney Gage, *ReThink Life: How to Live Different from the Norm* (Bloomington, IN: WestBow Press, 2013).

My instructor told me that when the red light turned green, it was "show time." I prayed the green light bulb would be burned out so we'd have to abort the jump as my instructor latched his tandem harness to mine. Suddenly, the light turned green and the side door was opened. I felt the powerful rush of wind and heard the deafening noise of plane engines and wind filling the cabin. When the instructor said it was time, we worked our way to the door. On the count of three, I did something I never thought I would ever do: I jumped!

I'll never forget the rush of that moment, the intense noise of my jumpsuit flapping in my ears, and the powerful sensation of rushing wind in my face. After a few moments of the craziness of falling mixed with the euphoria of floating in the air, my instructor pulled the ripcord. In an instant, we went from the penetrating noise of the rushing wind to the total tranquility of being suspended by a parachute thousands of feet in the air. Floating in the air above the clouds was one of the most incredible experiences of my life.

Strapped to my back, my instructor pointed out landmarks on the ground below. Everything was incredibly beautiful and peaceful as we looked across the horizon from ten thousand feet in the air. I was seeing the world below me from a completely different perspective, as if I were viewing God's creation from His perspective in high definition.

Sometimes we have to do something drastic to get above the noise and craziness of life. We're not implying that you need to jump out of a plane! We just need to do something drastic enough to break up the mundane routines of life. New experiences stimulate our creativity. If we don't have them, we'll lose our passion and purpose for living. Our mission, vision, and values for our marriage and family can get lost.

The pressures of this world can be overwhelming at times, but when we're tethered to God and direct our attention toward His plans and purposes for our lives, everything comes into focus. Life takes on new meaning—we get our fire and passion back. That's why we have to live in tandem with our Creator who wants to navigate our lives. Like my instructor, God will help us land in the bull's eye of His targeted drop zone if we'll let Him.

The men who couldn't get their friend to Jesus because of the crowd decided to do something drastic: They tore a hole in the roof and lowered their friend on a mat right in the middle of the crowd in front of Jesus. If we want to restore the passion in our marriage and family relationships, we need to stop and ask ourselves this clarifying question: If you knew you had one month to live, how would you live your life?

This question helps us realize very quickly what's most important and who is most important in our lives.

The four guys knew this might be their last chance to get their friend to Jesus to be healed, so they did something drastic: They took the necessary actions to deal with the problems and remove the obstacles standing in the way. We encourage you to remove the obstacles in your life that are competing for your passion for God and your vision for your marriage and family.

Expect the Unexpected

Have you ever noticed that you can make plans, but sometimes things don't always go as planned? Craig Groeschel is a leadership expert who observes, "Sometimes the biggest blessings in life are on the other side of opposition."[53]

The men with the paralyzed friend knew where Jesus was going to be and when he was going to be there. However, they weren't expecting such a huge crowd. Instead of giving up and getting discouraged, they got creative. They lowered their friend in front of Jesus—which was very unexpected: "When Jesus saw their faith, he said, 'Friend, your sins are forgiven'" (Luke 5:20).

---

[53] Craig Groeschel, *Unstoppable: The Hidden Keys to Living a Life of Purpose, Passion, and Power* (Grand Rapids, MI: Zondervan, 2020), 58.

Because God is unpredictable, we have to allow him to interrupt our lives so we can expect the unexpected and know that God has a way of getting our attention when we begin to lose our passion and focus for what matters most.

Create "God Space"

Did you notice where the men in the story lowered their friend? It was "into the middle of the crowd, right in front of Jesus" (Luke 5:19). They created space that wasn't there before. We have to do the same thing in our busy lives. We have to create space for what's important—space in our time with God, our spouse, and our children. Nothing is more important than those relationships. The Bible teaches us that when we lose our passion, we need to do three things. First, remember the height from which we have fallen. Second, repent by admitting to God that we've drifted. And third, repeat. We need to go back and do the things we need to do to live with greater intention. King Solomon reminds us, "Reverence for God adds hours to each day" (Proverbs 10:27, TLB).

Keep a Constant Reminder

"[Jesus] said to the paralyzed man, 'I tell you, get up, take your mat and go home.' Immediately he stood up in front of them, took what he had been lying on and went home praising God" (Luke 5:24-25, author addition). Why did Jesus tell the man to take his mat and go home? We believe it was to serve to remind him of the miracle of healing and the new start God was giving him.

On a trip when we visited our family in Dallas, we got together at Michelle's sister's house for dinner and an evening of fun, and she introduced us to a fascinating concept. She had purchased a Maker Kit from myintent.org. The challenge is to identify "one word" that best describes your intent. It could be a word that describes a virtue, a challenge you want to overcome, what you're most passionate about, or your highest hopes. The goal is to capture your intent in one word and keep it visible to serve as a constant reminder.

I (Rodney) chose the word SHIFT. How about you? What would your word be? What's your intent? What do you want to see happen in your life, career, marriage, family, health, etc.? The bigger question may be: What shifts do you need to make to remove the obstacles that are robbing you of your passion? Whatever it is, make a keepsake to remind yourself of it daily.

Divine Design

Our passion isn't an abstract thing. God has made us to desire, want, and strive for something greater than ourselves. The word *enthusiasm* is a combination of two Greek words that mean "God within." Passion that is directed by God comes from within, implanted by the Holy Spirit and nurtured by reading the Scriptures, the encouragement of other believers, and our experiences of following Jesus. In the classic movie *Chariots of Fire*, Eric Liddell is a Scottish man who is training for the 100-meter race in the 1924 Olympic Games. His sister believes he needs to give up his dream of running in the games and leave to be a missionary in China. In a poignant conversation, she tries again to convince him, but he explains that running isn't a chore; it's a spiritual experience that delights God. Eric tells her, "When I run, I feel His pleasure."[54]

When do you feel God's pleasure? What do you enjoy doing? Where do you see the hand of God moving you and using you? Our talents and desires aren't the product of random events and biology. God has had His hand in every aspect of our lives, including our passions. In his letter to the Ephesians, Paul connects the dots between the grace of God, our calling, and our passions:

---

54 *Chariots of Fire*. Directed by Hugh Hudson. Written by Colin Welland. Enigma Productions. Warner Bros., 1981.

> *God saved you by his grace when you believed. And you can't take credit for this; it is a gift from God. Salvation is not a reward for the good things we have done, so none of us can boast about it. For we are God's masterpiece. He has created us anew in Christ Jesus, so we can do the good things he planned for us long ago.*
> *—Ephesians 2:8-10 (NLT)*

Did you get that? You're God's work of art—a masterpiece of His creation! You are designed for something far greater and more meaningful than the temporal things of this life. You were made to make an eternal difference. Your career is what you get paid for, but your calling is what you were made for. When our goals align with God's heart and our passions are unleashed by gratitude and desire, we operate in our "sweet spot" of motivation.

> *Your job as a parent isn't to push your child into greatness. Your job is to help pull greatness out of them.*
> —Rodney and Michelle Gage

Our experiences confirm (or challenge) our goals and passions. For instance, when we sit down with couples to help them find and follow God's will for their family, all the lights on our souls' dashboards are flashing green. We love to see them understand what God wants to do in them and in the lives of each of their children.

We encourage young people to try lots of avenues to explore their interests. Experimentation gives them valuable experience, eliminates some options, and focuses them on a few. As we get older, we probably have an idea of what rings our bells, gives us great joy, and makes a difference in the lives of others. But it's never too late to make a switch. Plenty of people who have been in a career or pursued interests for decades find the courage to go in a different direction. Working hard for something we don't care about is called stress. Working hard for something we love is called *passion*. Helping our kids learn this truth, especially during their high school years, will save them years of heartache and confusion.

PASSION AND PERSONALITY

There are over eight billion people on the planet today, and all of us are as unique as snowflakes, each with particular talents, desires, and experiences. We aren't the chance product of random connections of molecules. God has skillfully crafted each of us. In a beautiful psalm, David praises God:

You made all the delicate, inner parts of my body
and knit me together in my mother's womb.
Thank you for making me so wonderfully complex!
Your workmanship is marvelous—how well I know it.
You watched me as I was being formed in utter seclusion,
as I was woven together in the dark of the womb.
You saw me before I was born.
Every day of my life was recorded in your book.
Every moment was laid out
before a single day had passed. —Psalm 139:13-16 (NLT)

Since the time of the ancient Greeks, philosophers have identified personality traits and, more importantly, groups of traits that shape each person's desires, pursuits, and responses. For instance, some of us are energized by being with a group of people. That's where we come alive! But others who are in the same group feel drained and need to be alone to recharge their emotional batteries. Some of us gravitate toward accomplishing tasks by discipline and detail, and others want to accomplish tasks by involving people. Some are concrete thinkers and see everything in black and white, but others are abstract and see the complexity in every situation. Some value safety very highly, and others thrive on taking risks. There are many different inventories that help people identify their personality types.

We can eagerly recommend a number of inventories, such as the DISC, Myers-Briggs, Enneagram, StrengthsFinder, and others. We want to introduce you to a personality profile developed by our church. It identifies five basic personality types.[55] You will have fun with these within your family. In fact, you may even start referring to each member of the family by their unique "avatar." See if one of these sounds familiar:

Ninja		You are procedural, task-oriented, and detail-loving. You love being as thorough as possible and would rather be behind the scenes than in a crowd. People may never see the NINJA, but they know you were there by the trail of completion left behind you!
Mastermind		You are inspirational, motivating, and a team builder. You can see the big picture vision and rally everyone behind it. You love seeing people come together to accomplish a common goal. If you see a great team, you can bet there is a MASTERMIND behind it all!

---

55   The description of four benefits are adapted from "Reasons to Learn More about Your Personality Type," Kendra Cherry, *VeryWellMind*, September 23, 2018, https://www.verywellmind.com/reasons-to-learn-more-about-your-personality-type-4099388.

Trailblazer		You show ownership, initiative, and independence. You can tackle just about anything and love to figure out how to do things better. The TRAILBLAZER loves a challenge and will rise to it without fail every time!
Guardian		You are a protector, a cultivator, and you are compassionate. You watch out for the people around you and take care of their every need. The guardian is no wimp, though; just try to hurt those close to a GUARDIAN, and you'll get your behind kicked!
Social Genius		You are outgoing, friendly, and a networker. You love chatting it up with everybody and, naturally, make people feel at ease around you. People might say, "Every time with the SOCIAL GENIUS is like the first time"!

None of the personality types is better than another. They all have strengths, and they all have deficiencies. We've seen four specific benefits of using these inventories:

1) You'll understand why you relate to others easily or with difficulty.

One of the main benefits of these inventories is that we get to look in a mirror and see ourselves more objectively. We may have thought we had a particular trait, and the inventory and analysis confirm our suspicion or give us something else to consider. These tools also give us plenty of opportunities to talk to our spouses, kids, coworkers, and friends about our interactions with them.

We need to be careful to avoid pigeonholing people with labels, but labels can help us see people through clearer lenses. For instance, if you're an introvert, and your spouse is an extrovert, how each of you feels at parties is very different, and how you feel when you're alone is quite opposite. Understanding opens doors to communication, patience, kindness, and affection.

2) **You'll understand why you respond to situations the way you do.**

Some of us feel guilty that we need to take more time to make decisions than someone else, while others live spontaneously without guilt but may regret decisions later. When both people understand their bent, they'll realize one of them isn't tragically flawed and the other supremely virtuous—they're just different in the way they process information and make decisions. Quite often, when a couple or team discusses the analysis, they exclaim, "No wonder you responded to me like that!"

3) **You can position yourself to live out your passions and accomplish your purpose.**

We don't use a hammer when we need to drive a screw into the wall, and we don't insist on using a car when we're trying to cross the ocean to France. But some of us are square pegs trying desperately to fit into the round holes our parents or others have told us is our only option. God didn't create us to all be the same, and one of the adventures of life is discerning where we fit best.

4) **You'll be more understanding and patient when other people can't do what you can do.**

One of the most common problems in marriages is that each person was initially attracted to the differences in their spouse, but over time (sometimes not much time!), the wonder turns into disdain. Don't expect your math-challenged husband to do complicated calculations in his head. Give him a break . . . and a calculator. And don't demand that your wife make decisions with only half of the information. That's not how she operates—and if you're lucky, she won't bring up all the times your quick decision turned out to be a bomb!

You'll find the Avatar Personality Test in the appendix of this book. Feel free to use it with your family, friends, and anyone else. You can also take the digital version on our website at **www.thewinningfamily.com**.

Use the Avatar Personality Test or another one you and those you love want to use together, and dive into fun and meaningful discussions about why you think differently, make decisions in different ways, are energized by different things, and respond to conflict in different ways. What does all this have to do with passion? Quite a lot. A passion killer is feeling misunderstood, and when we feel that way long enough, we're flooded with self-doubt—and that's not a recipe for a full, purposeful life!

> *Figure out what you'd give your life for, and you'll know what to give your time to.*
> —Bob Goff[56]

God has told us that we're His masterpiece, and He promises to uniquely use each of us to accomplish what only we can do—for Him, for His purposes, and for the people around us. Discover who you are, what you are designed to be and do, and then do it with all your heart.

THINK ABOUT IT:

1) When and how have you seen passion rule people, inspire people, and shackle people?
2) Before you read this chapter, how would you have defined "ambition"? What makes ambition good, right, and noble? What makes it unhealthy or bad?

---

56   Bob Goff, *Love Does: Discover a Secretly Incredible Life in an Ordinary World* (Nashville, TN: Thomas Nelson, 2012), 213

3) How have you seen ambition wreck someone's life? (No names, please!) And who do you know who is a good example of ambition focused on God's goals?
4) Do you believe you're God's masterpiece? Why or why not?
5) Take some time to look over the personality profiles in this chapter. Which one best reflects your design? How will these profiles help you, your spouse, and your kids understand each other more deeply?
6) What are the benefits you anticipate as you talk to your spouse and family about their personalities?

DO IT:

Answer and discuss these questions as a family:
1) Have each person (who is old enough) take the Avatar Personality Test (or another one if you prefer), and then sit down to discuss what you've uncovered. Make sure the conversation is encouraging!

CHAPTER 9

TOUGHEN UP

GPS: GROW STRONGER THROUGH YOUR STRUGGLES

Your capacity for pain will determine your potential for growth!
—Brian Houston[57]

There are three kinds of people: those who are coming out of a difficult time, those who are in the middle of one right now, and those who will face difficulties in the future. If you don't have problems, you don't have a pulse. We all go through struggles.

THE STRUGGLE IS REAL

Several years ago, we faced a medical crisis with our son Luke, the youngest of our three children, and our world was rocked. Like most

---

57 Brian Houston, *Your Best Life: How to Dream Big, Live Better, and Influence the World* (Nashville, TN: Thomas Nelson, 2007).

families with children, we had a very busy schedule. Keeping up with our son's schedule alone kept us hopping. We took Luke to ball practice several nights a week and watched him play games on Saturday mornings. In the spring of that year, Luke began to complain of pain in his leg and knee. Because a ball had hit him in one of his practices, we thought he must have broken something, but X-rays revealed that nothing was broken. Still, he continued to experience pain and began to limp. Doctors wrote it off as "growing pains," but we weren't convinced. After a few months had passed, his limp became more severe, and the pain didn't go away.

A friend who is an orthopedist told us to bring Luke to his house one evening so he could take a look at his leg. After examining Luke, the doctor told us that he had a hunch about the diagnosis, but he would need an MRI to confirm it. When he saw the MRI of Luke's hip, our orthopedist friend confirmed that Luke had a rare hip disease called Perthes, in which the ball of the femur slowly dies. If left untreated, the ball can completely crush under the person's weight, causing major problems for a lifetime.

After much research, we found a world-renowned specialist in Perthes about an hour and a half away from our home. We immediately made an appointment, but we weren't prepared for the news we heard. The doctor felt that the best form of treatment for Luke wasn't traditional surgery or leg braces. He recommended that Luke be placed in a wheelchair for two to four years. There would be no running, jumping, or playing any sports. Needless to say, our world was turned upside-down.

I (Michelle) can remember walking out of the hospital that day, pushing Luke in a wheelchair and trying to hold back the tears as I saw other crippled children in their wheelchairs. I was sure we would never see the world the same again. It was heartbreaking to realize Luke would be immobilized during some of the most active years of his life. Gradually, we began to realize that God had a greater plan for our son and for our family. Even though we didn't understand this plan at the time, we knew God was ultimately in control.

For nearly three years, Luke was in a wheelchair. Over the course of those years, many people told us that Luke's life was an inspiration to them as they went through their own personal struggles and challenges. Today, thanks to answered prayer and God's healing, Luke is out of his wheelchair and completely healed, but his healing is only part of the story. Luke has a clearer, deeper perspective about life now because of what he went through during those years. He sees difficult situations and physically challenged individuals with a different set of eyes. Our whole family has learned from this experience. It forced us to stop the drift into rampant pessimism and shift our focus to what's most important. We learned that God wants to use our struggles to fulfill His greater purposes—to use them for our benefit, and also the benefit of others.

We can't control what happens to us, but we can choose how we respond when we face difficult situations. Keeping the right perspective in the midst of our struggles is the key to overcoming our problems.

We've often shared a particular passage of Scripture with people who face difficulties. James, the half-brother of Jesus, begins his letter to Christians very abruptly ... and quite surprisingly. He wrote, "Consider it pure joy, my brothers and sisters, whenever you face trials of many kinds" (James 1:2).

How would you like to get an email from a friend with a subject line that reads: "Got Problems?" and when you click to open it, the first line says, "Just be happy!" I don't know about you, but when I'm facing struggles, the last thing I want to hear is encouragement to be happy in my pain! My first impression is to say, "How insensitive! How in the world do you expect me to be happy when you don't understand my situation?"

Thankfully, the verse doesn't stop there. It reads, "Consider it pure joy, my brothers, whenever you face trials of many kinds because you know that the testing of your faith develops perseverance." The key to this kind of response is "because you know." What, then, do we need to know to respond to difficulties with faith, confidence, and even joy?

FOUR "FACTS OF LIFE"

1) Struggles are inevitable.

It's not a matter of if but when we'll face struggles. It may be our health, finances, marriage, kids, job, or something else. You name it, we face it. James doesn't say, "If you encounter problems, consider it joy," but "whenever." In other words, count on it; you're going to have struggles. Jesus told His followers, "In this world you will have struggles" (John 16:33). And the apostle Peter wrote, "Do not be surprised at the fiery ordeal that has come on you to test you" (1 Peter 4:12). In other words, count on it. Problems aren't an elective class that we don't have to take. They're a required course. You don't get out of them by saying you don't want them. No one is exempt!

2) Struggles are unpredictable.

Our oldest daughter, Becca, is a singer and worship leader. During her first two years in college, she had the opportunity to travel with a worship team and to lead worship on the Liberty Worship Collective, which is the largest college worship gathering in the world. As a vocalist, your voice is your most important instrument. At one point, Becca began to notice she was struggling with her voice. Her voice began to grow raspy and hoarse. She was struggling to hit certain notes, and soon, others noticed too. She went to several doctors. At first, they thought she might have strep throat or mono; however, she didn't have the normal symptoms that come with strep or mono. Months went by, and her condition continued to grow worse.

We'll never forget when she came home during her Christmas break. She wasn't herself. One evening, as we were talking about her situation, she blurted out with tears coming down her face, "I don't know what's going on with me." She felt deeply discouraged. After multiple misdiagnoses, we were finally able to get her in to see an ear, nose, and throat specialist while she was home over her break. The doctor works with some of the top singers in the country. After some tests, he was able to pinpoint her problem: She had a yeast infection that had covered her vocal cords. The doctor told us that it was a very serious injury to her vocal cords, equivalent to an athlete tearing an ACL. She was immediately placed on vocal rest. Since then, God has healed her and fully restored her voice, and today, she's a worship leader at one of the largest churches in the country. She sings in front of thousands of people every week!

Becca's problem seemed to come out of nowhere. It's very common—we seldom see our struggles coming. They're unpredictable. James reminds us when he says, "whenever you face problems." The word "face" in Greek is *peripipto*, which literally means "to fall into unexpectedly." That's what makes a problem a problem.

3) Struggles come in different shapes and sizes.

We seldom get bored with the struggles we face because there are a wide variety of them. Have you ever tried to match paint shades on your walls to samples in the store? The Greek word for "many kinds" is literally translated "multicolored." Our struggles come in many shades and varieties. They vary in intensity, in variety, and in duration. Some are minor inconveniences, and some are catastrophic. Some of our struggles were custom-made to teach us things we would have never learned any other way.

4) Struggles are purposeful.

There's purpose in our pain. Struggles can teach us a lot if we'll let them. C. S. Lewis once said that, essentially, God speaks to us in our pleasures, but He shouts to us in our pain.[58] James explains that there are three purposes for the struggles we face:

- *They purify us.*

James uses the word "testing," as in testing gold and silver. A goldsmith heats gold and silver until all the impurities are burned off. In Job 23:10, it says, "He has tested me through the refining fire and I have come out as pure gold." Trials test our faith and purify us. Faith develops when things don't go as we planned and when we don't feel like doing what we know is right. Struggles can make us like steel—when we're tested, we come out stronger. Someone once asked a silversmith, "How do you know when the silver is pure?" He responded, "When I can see my reflection it." How do we know when we've learned the lessons God is teaching us through our struggles? When God can see His reflection in us, He knows we've been refined.

> *Life can grind you down or polish you up. . . It all depends on what you're made of.*
> *—Zig Ziglar*[59]

- *They give us endurance.*

James says that "the testing of your faith develops perseverance." He's talking about staying power and endurance—the ability to keep on keeping on, the ability to hang in there. The Greek translation here means "the ability to stay under pressure." We don't like pressure, and we do everything we can to avoid it. In fact, most people attempt to escape from it through sleeping pills, drugs, alcohol, entertainment, food, etc. But God uses problems and struggles in our lives to teach us how to handle pressure, so we never give up.

---

58 C. S. Lewis, *The Problem of Pain* (New York, NY: HarperOne, 2001), 93.
59 Zig Ziglar, *Zig: The Autobiography of Zig Ziglar* (Nashville, TN: Thomas Nelson, 2002), 207.

How does God teach you patience? By everything not going your way. He even teaches us patience in bumper-to-bumper traffic, in grocery lines, when we're with annoying people, and when we have to wait.

- *They help us grow.*

Struggles can make us stronger and become more like Jesus because they help us grow and mature. James wrote that "the testing of your faith produces perseverance that you may be mature and complete, not lacking anything" (James 1:4). That's God's long-range goal for your life, marriage, and family relationships. The ultimate purpose is maturity, so that we would gradually become more like Jesus. God is much more interested in building our character than in making us comfortable.

Through our struggles, God has a way of turning it all around for our good if we'll let Him. One of the most-quoted passages in the Bible is Romans 8:28 [author addition]: "We know that all things work together for good" [not all things are good, but they work together for good] if we love God and are called according to His purpose."

It's a lot like making chocolate cake. When you read the instructions on how to make chocolate cake, it first tells you what ingredients you need: eggs, milk, butter, unsweetened cocoa, baking soda, baking powder and vanilla, etc. However, if you eat raw eggs by themselves, they're horrible. No one eats a stick of butter by itself (well, some might), no one eats baking soda by itself, and . . . you get the point! However, when you mix it all together, put it in the oven, and let it bake, what do you get? A delicious chocolate cake. That's what God wants to do when he allows us to experience struggles. God can take something bitter and make it better. The next time you and your spouse go through struggles or one of your children faces hardships in school or friendships, remember to turn the "i" into "e"—this shift allows our struggles to make us *better* rather than *bitter*.

> *The one who is in you is GREATER than what you are going through.*
> —Rodney Gage

TAKEAWAYS

God never wastes a hurt. There's purpose even in our pain. The opening story in this chapter concerning our son Luke allowed him to learn an incredible lesson. He learned that if he hadn't gone through being in a wheelchair for nearly three years, he may have never learned what his greatest strength was. It was while he was in a wheelchair that he discovered his passion for music. During that time when he wasn't very mobile, he learned to play the guitar and keyboard. Today, he's a singer, songwriter, photographer, video editor, whiz with technology, and a freakishly talented musician. He found his greatest strengths through one of his greatest struggles. Only God can take what the enemy meant for harm and turn it around for the good.

> *Success is to be measured not so much by the position that one has reached in life as by the obstacles which he has overcome.*
> —Booker T. Washington[60]

Of course, it's no fun to go through struggles, but God allows us to go through them so that we will ultimately depend upon him and grow in every area of our lives. It's through our weaknesses that God can show His strength and power. Peter reminds us:

> *Don't be surprised at the fiery trials you are going through, as if something strange were happening to you. Instead, be very glad— for these trials make you partners with Christ in his suffering, so that you will have the wonderful joy of seeing his glory when it is revealed to all the world. . . . So if you are suffering in a manner that pleases God, keep on doing what is right, and trust your lives*

---

60   Booker T. Washington, *Up from Slavery* (New York, NY: Doubleday, Page & Co., 1901), 28

to the God who created you, for he will never fail you. —1 Peter 4:12-13, 19 (NLT)

Through our struggles, we craft a story that God will use to comfort and inspire others. It's a law of life: Only those who have walked in our shoes have the credibility to speak words of truth and life to us, and only when we've learned to trust God through our struggles will we be able to impart courage to the people around us—particularly those who watch us most closely, our spouse and children.

We want to leave you with two crucial takeaways:

Find the Greater Purpose

Instead of asking the question "Why?" ask "What now?"

- What is it that God is teaching me through my painful circumstances?
- How can I grow from them?
- How can I allow the struggles in our marriage to bring greater patience and understanding in our relationship?
- How can I teach my children to grow stronger through their struggles?
- What hidden strengths is God showing me through these times of difficulty?
- How can we profit from our problems as a family?

If we look hard enough, we can always find a greater purpose through our pain and problems. God has a way of directing us, inspecting us, and perfecting us. In working with many couples and families through the years, we've learned that they have a difficult time seeing the good in all the bad. It's easy to get overwhelmed with all the bad, but in these times, our greatest purposes are often revealed. Is God trying to direct you? Maybe God is allowing the struggles in your life right now to get your attention and direct your path. Maybe you're standing at a fork in the road right now, and you're trying to make some important decisions concerning your future? Maybe God is using the struggles of one of your children to reveal His greater purpose in her life. God uses both the good and the bad to get our attention. Maybe God wants you to take some time to inspect what's going on in your situation. Are you overlooking something important? What is God preparing you for? Having been married for almost thirty-five years, we've learned that God uses us in each season of our lives, but before we enter the next season, God wants to prepare us by perfecting us.

In his book *Necessary Endings*, Dr. Henry Cloud talks about how the good can't begin until the bad ends.[61] Life is about endings and new beginnings. Life has seasons, stages, and phases. This is what growth is about. If there is no growth, we become stagnant. Getting to the next level always means leaving something behind and moving forward. Some endings are natural, and some are forced. Cloud uses the illustration of a rose bush to teach us that we have to prune things that are toxic, dead, or unwanted. A rose bush only has enough resources to feed so many buds to their full potential. It can't bring all of them into full bloom. In order for the bush to thrive, a certain number of buds have to go. Some of the buds are good but not the best. Some are sick and not getting well, and there are ones that have long been dead. The caretaker carefully and regularly examines those that need to be pruned, and he makes the cuts.

If we accept the premise that pruning is necessary, but have a great deal of emotional discomfort about it, we'll struggle to realize our potential. We need to understand that endings are normal and change our mindset so that we accept them and even welcome them. If we see our struggles as normal and expected, we can let God use them to direct us, inspect us, and perfect us. God always has a greater purpose for our struggles.

---

61 Henry Cloud, *Necessary Endings: The Employees, Businesses, and Relationships That All of Us Have to Give Up in Order to Move Forward* (New York: HarperBusiness, 2010).

Find a Way to Help Others Through Their Struggles

It's easy to sit around in self-pity or blame others for the problems we face, but at some point, we have to take the focus off ourselves and place it on others. God allows pain so we can learn from our struggles. In fact, overcoming our struggles is a big part of our story. It doesn't take long to discover someone else who's dealing with bigger problems than ours. The legendary basketball coach John Wooden once said, "You can't live a perfect day without doing something for someone who will never be able to repay you."[62] Who better to encourage someone who has been diagnosed with cancer than someone who has had cancer? Who better to encourage someone who has experienced the pain of divorce than someone who has gone through it themselves? Who better to give hope and help to someone going through financial difficulties than someone who has lost everything? You get the point. There are always people who are waiting to be helped with the comfort and care that only those who've experienced their struggle can give. Sally Koch once said, "Great opportunities to help others seldom come, but small ones surround us daily."[63]

Remember, every family ends up somewhere, but few families end up somewhere on purpose. Follow your GPS—your goals, passions, and lessons from your struggles. No matter where you've come from and what hurdles you still need to jump over, you can make the shift. You can trust Him to be there every step of the way!

---

62 John Wooden, *They Call Me Coach* (New York, NY: Bantam Books, 1972), 57.

63 Sally Koch, "Great opportunities to help others seldom come, but small ones surround us daily," quoted in *Pass It On*, Foundation for a Better Life, accessed May 13, 2025, https://www.passiton.com/inspirational-quotes/3700-sally-koch.

THINK ABOUT IT:
1) Do you agree or disagree with the statement that our struggles can make us bitter or better? Explain your answer.
2) Struggles are inevitable, unpredictable, come in many shapes and sizes, and are purposeful. What did you learn about struggles from this chapter? What kind of struggles are you facing right now?
3) Which of the three ways God wants to use struggles in our lives have you experienced? Explain your answer.
4) Could God be using your current circumstances and struggles to direct you, inspect you or perfect you? Which one of these do you think He is using right now in your life, marriage, or family relationships?
5) What is the story God wants to tell through your struggles? What's holding you back from sharing that story? Who do you know right now God wants you to encourage? Or if you're currently facing a struggle, take a deep dive into how you might use this struggle as part of a story to tell others when you've overcome it.
6) What areas of growth do you need to help your kids with? Taking their goals, passions, and struggles into consideration, is there a hidden strength that God wants to use for His greater purpose?
7) What did you learn from the illustration of the rose bush? What needs to be pruned in your life?

DO IT:
Answer and discuss these questions as a family:
1) Think of one person who's struggling right now (it may be the person sleeping next to you or down the hall). With grace and empathy, step into that person's life to show you care. Talk little and listen much.

STEP 4

FIND LIFE-GIVING FRIENDSHIPS

A SHIFT IN REINFORCEMENT

CHAPTER 10

IRON SHARPENS IRON

TEACH YOUR KIDS TO KNOW THE DIFFERENCE BETWEEN COMPANIONS AND CONFIDANTS

God gives us our relatives—thank God we can choose our friends.
—Ethel Watts Mumford[64]

Have you ever used jumper cables before? If you haven't, you've likely seen someone else use them to help jump-start another vehicle with a dead battery. Recently, my (Rodney's) car wouldn't start, so I asked a friend to pull his vehicle up next to mine so the jumper cables would reach both our cars. My friend opened up the hood and told me to go ahead and

---

64 Ethel Watts Mumford, quoted in *The Yale Book of Quotations*, ed. Fred R. Shapiro (New Haven: Yale University Press, 2006), 540.

latch the cables onto the battery of my car. After I put the red (positive) and the black (negative) cables onto my car's correct battery terminals, my friend proceeded to put his end of the cables onto his battery terminals. However, I noticed he was getting ready to clamp the (black) negative cable onto the (red) positive terminal. Quickly, I shouted, "Wait! Don't put the negative onto the positive!" My terrified friend asked, "Why? What difference will it make?" I said, "If you have the negative on the positive and start your engine, it can damage the engine and potentially cause the battery to burst!"

When you think about it, the same is true with friendships. Our friends are either a plus or a minus. Negative influence can cause serious problems in our lives if we're not careful. Nothing can cause us to drift faster and further away from our mission and vision for our marriage and family than negative influences. If we get our friendships right, our friends can help set us up for success in every area of our lives. The opposite is also true: If we get our friendships wrong, the wrong friends can set us up for a whole lot of pain, regret, disappointment, or even destruction. As the old saying goes, "Show me your friends and I will show you your future." As we move into the fourth step of our 5-Step Plan to stop the drift and start living with greater intention, there is another shift we need to make. It's what we call the shift in reinforcement. Without a clear vision for our future, strong moral values we hold in our hearts, and an understanding of how to use our GPS, we are vulnerable to what my pastor friend Ed Young calls the "sway of they."[65]

If we're insecure about who we are and what we believe on the inside, our temptation and vulnerability is to cave in to the pressures from the outside. The norm is to conform to the path of popularity. This is what most parents fear the most—a child or teenager conforming to the negative influences of their peers and popular culture. That's why the apostle Paul warned, "Do not be misled: 'Bad company corrupts good character'"

---

[65] Ed Young, "The Sway of 'They,'" sermon/article, Fellowship Church, May 20, 2018, EdYoung.com.

(1 Corinthians 15:33). As parents, one of the most important gifts we can give our kids is the wisdom to pick good friends. We make a huge mistake when we assume "they'll find good friends." Yes, they may, but it's our responsibility to steer them toward life-giving friendships. But before we focus on them, let's talk about you and me. One of the greatest impacts we can have on our kids is to show them the power of choosing the right kind of friendships. What kind of friends do you currently associate with? What kind of values do they have? What kind of influence do they have on your marriage, family, and the choices you make? According to business icon and entrepreneur Jim Rohn, "you are the average of the five people you spend the most time with."[66] If that statement is true, on a scale of one to ten, how would you rate yourself with the five people you and your spouse spend the most time with? How are they influencing you on a professional, spiritual, financial, parental, and relational level? Here is a motto we have found to be very true that can affect us in a positive way or a negative way:

>Where you go determines who you meet.
>Who you meet determines how you think.
>How you think determines what you do.
>What you do determines who you become.

REFRAMING FRIENDSHIPS

In the blink of an eye, the popular concept of friendship has changed. According to an article in *Live Science*, the average American today only has two close friends, while only twenty-five years ago, the average American reported having six. Even more alarming is that one in four report not having a single close and trusted friend.[67] I believe friendships are under stress for three main reasons: longer work hours due to sending

---

66 Jack Canfield and Janet Switzer, *The Success Principles: How to Get from Where You Are to Where You Want to Be* (New York: HarperCollins, 2005), epigraph, credited to Jim Rohn.

67 Jeanna Bryner, "Close Friends Less Common Today, Study Finds," *Live Science*, November 4, 2011, https://www.livescience.com/16879-close-friends-decrease-today.html.l

and responding to emails long after leaving the office, rising divorce rates that rupture networks of relationships, and the explosion of social media that has redefined what it means to be a "friend." Many people are obsessed with their online image and neglect real, face-to-face connections with people. Social media is no longer a supplement to relationships; it's a replacement.

In a message on friendships, Tim Keller said there are four crucial components: constancy, carefulness, candor, and counsel. *Constancy* is the commitment to be there for another person through thick and thin. In fact, when times are tough, real friends are even more present, more supportive, and more willing to sacrifice for their friend. *Carefulness* is discernment to "read" the friend in order to know what to say at any given moment. We don't just say what comes to mind; we carefully tailor our words to the person and the moment. But true friends tell each other the hard truth when they need to hear it. *Candor* is just as important as carefulness, and in fact, if it's not present, we might wonder if the two people are friends at all. *Counsel* is the ability to give advice and steer the person in a direction that's life-giving. Keller summarizes the four into two: A true friend always lets you in and never lets you down.[68]

Years ago, we met a young couple that were dating, and we really hit it off with them. We had a lot of interests in common. As we got to know them, we led her to Christ, and before long, I (Rodney) performed their wedding. We enjoyed seeing them grow in their relationships with each other and in their relationship with God. Before long, we became very close. They were among our closest friends and confidants. After a couple of years or so, Michelle and I sensed some distance in our relationship with them. We wondered what we'd done that might have offended them. We tried to talk to them, but they said, "Oh, there's no problem. Everything is fine." But we knew it wasn't.

---

68 imothy Keller, "Friendship: What It Is and Why It Matters," YouTube video, 1:04:20, posted by *The Gospel Coalition*, October 10, 2014, https://www.youtube.com/watch?v=8Tc4VIQrXdE.

After a few weeks, we discovered they had been hanging around some other couples and doing things they normally wouldn't do. We had been around the other couples before, and it caused us to become concerned about the negative influence those couples might have on our friends. It was a very toxic group of people who seemed to take delight in being critical and negative. We hoped to mend any rifts in the relationship, so we asked them to have coffee with us. As we talked, they informed us that they were leaving our church. We felt confused and frustrated. Maybe *betrayed* is a better word to describe our emotions. We had invested our time, hearts, and love in them. We'd walked with them through some serious storms in their lives, and now they were turning their backs on us. As we drove away from our visit with them, we were deeply hurt, confused, and, needless to say, disappointed that our friendship with them had come to an end.

Our children saw us walk through this difficult and painful season. We told them enough of what had happened, so they understood our shock and heartache. They felt our pain. We talked with them many times about whether we can trust people and if we can, how much and how fast. Our kids saw us feel the hurt, but they also saw us choose to forgive, refuse to take revenge by gossiping about the couple, and learn hard-won lessons about the value and vulnerability of friendships.

> *Your tribe determines your vibe.*
> —Rodney and Michelle Gage

As parents, we're imprinting images and values on our children from the time they're born. What they see is what they believe is good and right and normal. If they see resentment and estrangement, they'll believe all people are enemies and they should be suspicious of others. If they see apathy, they'll conclude that relationships aren't really important at all. But if they see genuine, strong, give-and-take friendships, they'll understand that choosing and building good friends is a crucial part of life. The message to them begins with us. The quality of our friendships has a dramatic impact on what our kids value in the people they choose as friends. As I mentioned earlier, the "sway of they" can be powerful and, at times, detrimental to us and our kids fulfilling our destinies. If we don't hold to strong beliefs and values on the inside, we will cave in to the pressures on the outside.

THE BAD NEWS

We know that the bodies of girls typically grow earlier than those of boys, but by mid-adolescence, the boys have caught up. Before long, both of them look like young adults, and parents usually expect them to act like young adults. But there's a problem. The prefrontal cortex of their brains continues to develop until they're about twenty-five years old. This is the part of the brain that is responsible for "executive function," reasoning that is essential for them to make good decisions. Before this part of the brain develops, they rely more on the amygdala, which is part of "the reptilian brain" and is associated with impulsive decisions, emotions, and instincts. In addition, the limbic system is also active in adolescents before the prefrontal cortex is fully developed. This part of the brain controls risk and reward. This combination of factors means teenagers naturally seek adventure, but they lack the ability to process information that adults interpret as stop signs. In other words, they live far more by impulse than they will later.

Neurobiologist Dr. Frances Jensen has studied the adolescent brain and recommends that parents realize their thinking patterns are different:

> *I think we need to remind ourselves that they're experiencing emotion in Technicolor, whereas we're experiencing it in black and white. And it makes you understand a bit more why they behave the way they do. Maybe you can count to 10 and not react. Back off and re-approach in a more organized way.*

[Teenage love] feels very real to the person in that moment. It's bona fide emotion; it's just not emotion that's measured like it will be later in life, where you might say, "I'm attracted to this person, but there's a lot of reasons why this may not be." It's real but just feels unbridled. Teens have superheated limbic systems, so the emotional areas, the sexual incentive areas, are on.[69]

This is why helping our kids choose the right associations and stay true to their core beliefs and values is so vital to helping them fulfill God's best for their lives.

THREE VITAL FRIENDSHIPS

Your kids need to see you investing in and enjoying three types of friendships: your friendship with God, your friendship with your spouse, and your friendships with a few other close companions. As they watch, they'll realize the value of each of these connections.

With God

It's a stunning fact that God, the infinite, omniscient, all-powerful Creator of the universe, wants the kind of relationship with us that can be called a friendship. On the night Jesus was arrested, He spent an extended time with His closest followers. They had heard Him teach and do miracles for over three years. Now, when it was time for Him to die, He wanted to leave them with important messages. He told them:

"I've told you these things for a purpose: that my joy might be your joy, and your joy wholly mature. This is my command: Love one another the way I loved you. This is the very best way to love. Put your life on the line for your friends. You are my friends when you do the things I command you. I'm no longer calling you servants because servants don't understand what their master is thinking

---

[69] Julia Scott, "Why is the Teenage Brain So Unpredictable? A Neurobiologist Explains," *PBS News*, May 24, 2017, https://www.pbs.org/newshour/health/teenage-brain-unpredictable-neurobiologist-explains.

and planning. No, I've named you friends because I've let you in on everything I've heard from the Father."—John 15:11-15 (MSG)

Do you relate to God as a friend? Many of us don't. Our relationship with God is, to a large extent, formed by our relationship with our parents. If they were harsh, we typically believe God is demanding and condemning. If they were distant, we usually believe God doesn't really care. But if they were fairly consistent in their affection, wisdom, and presence, we'll probably believe God cares, He's present, and we can trust Him.

With Your Spouse

Marriage can become stale. The rigors of juggling schedules, financial headaches, the constant demands of parenting, pressures from in-laws, and differences in sexual appetites can erode the joy and creativity of the first years of marriage until the two people are little more than roommates—roommates who barely tolerate each other. Studies by Dr. John Gottman show that of all the facets of a marriage relationship, the one that is the most significant predictor of a healthy marriage is friendship.[70] Enjoying and trusting each other oils the complex mechanism of competing schedules, desires, and expectations. Bill Hanawalt, executive pastor of the Vineyard Christian Church in Evanston, Illinois, observes:

Marriage without friendship cannot work in our culture. Friendship has to be nourished and nurtured regularly or it faces the danger of becoming a business relationship. I have seen many distant and business-like marriages where careers have developed and children have come into the picture, and the priority of emotional connection has been left to die on the vine. Couples that don't give attention to developing their friendship often come apart. It also creates an opening for marital infidelity.[71]

---

70 Liz Higgins, "5 Simple Ways to Strengthen Your Marriage," *The Gottman Institute*, December 19, 2016.

71 Glenn T. Stanton, "The Role of Friendship in Marriage: My Best Friend, My Spouse," *Focus on the Family*, https://www.focusonthefamily.com/marriage/sex-and-intimacy/the-role-of-friendship-in-marriage/the-role-of-friendship-in-marriage-my-best-friend-my-spouse.

To continue to build a strong friendship in marriage, each person needs to invest time, energy, and heart. Little things matter: Pay attention when the other is talking, stimulate the other person's creativity, do chores together, forgive offenses (real or imagined), and make the relationship a priority rather than taking it for granted.

With Others

Solomon gives the clearest, most succinct commentary on the power of relationships we've ever seen: "Walk with the wise and become wise; associate with fools and get in trouble" (Proverbs 13:20, NLT). We see it all the time. When we spend time with people who are pursuing God and His purposes with all their hearts, their passion rubs off on us. And when we spend time with people who value success, pleasure, and approval more than anything, their perspective awakens discontent, comparison, and unhealthy competition.

Some of us are from families that have crippled us emotionally and relationally. We bear the scars of years of harm. For a few, the damage came like hammer blows, but for others, constant criticism wore away our self-confidence like sandpaper on a pine board. We may have had painful relationships with those we counted on in the past, but God can give us a new family, His family. Again, we turn to Solomon, who wrote: "There are 'friends' who destroy each other, but a real friend sticks closer than a brother" (Proverbs 18:24, NLT). I know a lot of people who can testify to this truth. They have felt abandoned or abused in their childhoods, but they've found new brothers and sisters in the church. Of course, not everyone who comes to church can be a true friend. Church is full of broken people, sinful people, people who have suffered from "destroyed" relationships for any number of reasons. But church is also the place where God does deep work in our hearts, where wounds are healed, wisdom is imparted, and trust is gradually built. These friends are with us in our darkest times, and they don't laugh, run away, or give us simplistic answers to life's deepest problems.

LAYERS OF FRIENDSHIPS

In our lives and, we suspect, in yours, it's easy to identify three distinct layers of friendships: surface, structured, and secure. We can know someone for years but never connect beyond a *surface* level. We talk about the weather, or a sports team, or something happening in town, but we don't move below the level of facts. We may have hundreds or even thousands of connections like this.

We have a deeper level of connections with people who have shared interests with us. These are *structured* relationships. We're in a club, we work together, our kids are on the same team, or we play tennis with them. These people have at least some idea of what we value, and they affirm what we believe. They're cheerleaders when we do well, and they overlook most of our faults. We may have dozens of these people in our lives.

A third layer is those who give us *security*. We've moved beyond facts and shared interests—we have shared hearts. We delight in the same things, and we grieve over the same losses. These are the people who show up at the worst moments of our lives, and these are the people who celebrate our successes instead of feeling threatened by our progress. We don't have many friends like this, and we don't need many—maybe two or three at a time.

Today, social media has changed our definition of "friends." We may have thousands of friends on Facebook and a similar number on Instagram, but we carefully craft the "face" we let people see. We do more posing than sharing. There's nothing wrong with these superficial connections as long as they're not the only kind we have. If we fail to go to the two deeper levels, we'll assume that the number of likes tells us how many true friends we have, and we'll miss out on authentic, soul-nourishing connections with a few people.

> *Choose friends who celebrate you, not tolerate you.*
> —Ed Young[72]

Our circle of friends usually changes as we enter new stages of life or move to new communities. And sometimes, our interests change, so we gain new friends around the new endeavors. In their book, *Relationships*, psychologists Les and Leslie Parrott identify "friends of the road" and "friends of the heart." They explain:

> *With most friendships, new concerns and new faces gradually crowd out the old as we start a new journey. But not with committed friends. They don't flicker and fade; they keep the lights on. They are there for the duration and are as elemental to our being as blood to our heart.*
>
> *Are friendships of the heart more important than our fleeting friends of the road? Not really. We need both. What matters is how a relationship sustains you right now. An achieved friendship—of any brand or bond—is among the best experiences life has to offer.*[73]

> *We may impress people with our strengths but we connect with our weaknesses.*
> —Craig Groeschel[74]

MENDING THE BROKEN PLACES

Some of the most painful times in our lives occur when we experience conflict with people we love and trust. All significant relationships are messy from time to time, so we need to understand how to mend them when they're broken. The cause of the fracture may be any number of

---

72 Ed Young, *Outrageous, Contagious Joy* (Dallas, TX: The Ed Young Ministries, 2005), 112.
73 Les and Leslie Parrott, *Relationships* (Grand Rapids, MI: Zondervan, 1998), 79.
74 Craig Groeschel, *The Christian Atheist: Believing in God but Living As If He Doesn't Exist* (Grand Rapids, MI: Zondervan, 2010), 78.

things, including unrealistic expectations on the part of one person, leading to the other feeling smothered; the clash of political perspectives; differences of opinion about raising children; one person moving to another city; busyness that gradually causes the friendship to cool; and the dagger thrust of betrayal.

We probably have no need to mend broken relationships on the superficial level because there's not enough emotional vulnerability to expose us to hurt. On the structured layer, however, shared interests can lead to sharp disagreements. A shared purpose can unite us, but different strategies can divide us. The measure of hurt in relationships is directly proportional to the level of trust. When we're vulnerable, we share what's in our hearts, which can be wonderfully healing or terribly damaging. Let us offer some suggestions for healing the fractures in any significant relationship:

Be Honest with Yourself

Many people let hurt turn into anger, which then turns into bitterness, all because they don't want to admit they're hurt. Denial never leads to healing and reconciliation. Before we find the courage and the right words to talk to the other person, we need to take time for some self-reflection. If the pain is overwhelming, it's wise to get the comfort and advice of someone who has been down this road before and found hope and healing along the way.

Prepare for the Talk

We often make one of two mistakes when we try to resolve a disagreement: We run in too quickly, or we hesitate too long. We need a combination of good preparation and plenty of courage. Before talking to the person, carefully think out what you want to say and how you want to say it. Try to see the issue from the other person's point of view so you can empathize. Try to find common ground, and realize the person will almost certainly have a different point of view. You'll have to decide, before the conversation, how much to push back and how much to let go. Don't set the time to talk until you're prepared. (It's usually wise to bounce your plan off someone who is wise and objective.)

Speak Up, Speak Respectfully

When we wade in to talk to someone about a problem in a relationship, some of us use intimidation to get our way, and some just want to get the talk over as soon as possible. If we're prepared, we can say what we planned to say, and then listen to the response. Our goal isn't to force them to agree with us (that's manipulation), but to find some common ground so we can make progress in the relationship. It's wise to begin by sharing your painful feelings: "I feel hurt," "I feel angry," or "I feel afraid." Then describe the problem, try to empathize, "You probably see it this way . . ." and then say, "I want us to have a healthier relationship. Here are some steps we can take." Or you might say, "Here are some steps *I'm* going to take."

Don't Expect Instant Resolution

Sometimes, when we bring up hard things to someone, they respond very well and immediately—but that's very rare. Far more often, they're defensive or evasive. Expect this kind of response, and give the person time to think about it before you talk again in a day or two.

Forgive

Forgiveness is unilateral, but reconciliation takes both. In other words, we can forgive the person who hurt us whether she ever admits the wrong or ever changes. We forgive because Jesus has forgiven us (Ephesians 4:32), but we're foolish to trust someone who hasn't proven to be trustworthy. Reconciliation usually takes time, and it can't happen until and unless the other person admits the wrong, genuinely grieves the pain she has caused, and makes a commitment (and follows through) to never do it again.

> *It is in forgiving that one is forgiven.*
> —Mother Teresa[75]

Rebuild Trust

Some fractures in relationships are minor and can be repaired fairly soon. In fact, when they're over, we wonder why we didn't resolve it sooner! But others involve severe breaches of trust and years of lies and wounds. These require plenty of time and hard work on both sides for the relationship to be rebuilt. The good news is that if both people are willing, God can do amazing things.

A woman came to talk to me (Rodney) after a divorce. I listened as the wife told me about her husband putting his time and heart into his career and spending very little time with her or their children. She was heartbroken. I asked if her ex would come with her next time. He agreed, and again she told her story about his lack of interest in her and the children. To my surprise, he wasn't defensive, and he didn't blame her. He nodded to affirm that all she was saying was true. His honesty was a huge open door for reconciliation!

I met with him several times. He trusted in Christ and started attending our church. In time, his agenda, life's mission, vision, and values were radically transformed. During all this, I gave him some specific things to do to rekindle the relationship. He took his former wife on dates, and he made the reservations. He called her during the day to tell her he loved her, and they soon invited their kids to go to dinner and other activities with them. Her heartache was healed by his authentic and consistent displays of love. Months later, he called to ask me to perform their second marriage. It was a wonderful restoration of what selfishness had broken.

---

75 Mother Teresa, *The Simple Path* (New York, NY: BlueBridge, 2003), 45.

She was finally cherished and safe, and the kids had a loving, attentive father for the first time in their lives. All this started because she came to me with a broken heart.

Depending on the nature of the relationship, we don't necessarily have to reconstruct the same level of trust and vulnerability as we had before the relationship was strained. We need to weigh the benefits and count the costs. Some connections are so valuable that we'll do anything to repair them, but many, especially in the structured category, aren't high enough on our priority list to take time away from our most important relationships to do the time-consuming work of rebuilding. Even then, it's our responsibility to forgive, to speak kindly of the person, and to drift gently apart with no animosity.

> *When the right people come into your life, you'll understand why the wrong ones had to leave.*
> —Rodney Gage

What does all this have to do with families? Everything! If our children see us avoiding hard conversations, they'll believe they aren't competent to resolve the struggles they have with people. Then, the two options are fight or flight—demanding and intimidating others or hiding physically or emotionally. But if they see us enjoying our most important relationships and doing the hard work to keep them strong, they'll learn valuable lessons about the importance of great friendships . . . and they'll make a crucial shift toward becoming wise adults.

THINK ABOUT IT:
1) How would you paraphrase this statement: "True friends always let you in and never let you down"?
2) What is your level of fear about your children developing healthy friendships? Explain your answer.
3) Describe your relationships with God, your spouse, and a few of your best friends. Are any improvements needed in each area?
4) How would you evaluate the quality and quantity of your three layers of friends: surface, structured, and secure?
5) As you've observed friendships over the years, what factors have caused the most strains and fractures?
6) How confident are you in taking steps to try to reconcile relationships that have been broken?
7) Why is it important to differentiate forgiveness from trust and reconciliation?
8) What do your children see when they watch you and your friends?

DO IT:
Answer and discuss these questions as a family:
1) Have a conversation with your spouse and talk about your most encouraging and your most painful friendships.
2) Have a conversation with your kids and tell them about your best friends and those that weren't so positive. (Let your descriptions be age-appropriate.)

CHAPTER 11

EVERY FRIENDSHIP NEEDS A LITTLE TLC

CONSIDER CHARACTER WHEN CHOOSING FRIENDS

You can tell more about a person by what he says about others than you can by what others say about him.
—Anonymous

Not too long ago, as I (Rodney) was grilling on our back porch, I heard a very unusual sound. I opened the screen door and saw an owl in a big bush outside. I ran inside and grabbed Michelle and the kids. I didn't want to scare the bird, so I whispered as loud as I could, "Y'all come out to see this...and be real quiet!" When they joined me on the porch, I pointed to the owl in the bush, but none of them saw it. It was right there in front of them, but they couldn't see it. I pointed and described it until Michelle and the kids could see the big, beautiful bird. It had been in plain sight all along! We stood in silence and amazement. There's no telling how long this wonderful creature had been sitting quietly in the bush next to our door. We could have enjoyed it sooner if we had known where to look.

Owls are interesting creatures. In our part of the country, and especially in our neighborhood, they're rare, and they're difficult to see because they blend into their natural habitat. Usually, someone else has to point them out and say, "Look—there it is!" But when owls hoot, it's unmistakable. Their sound is a sure sign one of them is nearby. Wise people are like this owl. They usually blend in with the crowd. They may be still and quiet for a long time as they observe what is going on around them, but when they speak up, everyone else knows they've heard the sound of true wisdom. Solomon, one of the wisest men who ever lived, was right when he said in Proverbs 13:20, "Walk with the wise and become wise, for a companion of fools suffers harm." One of the wisest things we can do from time to time is to take what we call a "friendatory." Ask yourself the question, How is my friending trending? As we learned in the previous chapter, our friends are either a plus or a minus. They are either inspiring us to reach our full potential or causing us to drift. If we want to avoid drifting away from the things that matter most in our lives, we need to surround our-selves with wise people. Like the owl, wise people are not always easy to recognize at first. They tend not to draw a lot of attention to themselves. We have learned from our own experiences with friendships that a few characteristics stand out among wise friends. We call these the TLC of friendship. Wise friends are tough, loyal, and committed.

TOUGH

In the summer before I (Rodney) entered the seventh grade, our family moved from Houston to Dallas. My parents knew I wanted to find some new friends, so they introduced me to the son of a couple they knew. Beasley and I became great friends, and he helped me make the transition to a new city, a new school, and a lot of new kids. He was highly respected for his athletic skills and because he was strong in his commitment to Christ. As school started, he took me under his wing and made me feel accepted. He set me up for success in relationships, which, as you undoubtedly know, is quite a challenge for a new kid in junior high school.

One day in the locker room, the older boys were harassing the younger kids like me. They used their size and numbers to intimidate us, and they even hoisted us up and hung us by our belt loops on hooks on the wall. When they came at me, Beasley walked in, saw what was happening, and stood between the boys and me. He told them, "If you want to get him, you'll have to go through me! You're not going to treat my friend that way!" At that moment, he could have turned around and walked out without saying a word, or he could have joined them in intimidating me, but he stood up for me at the risk of his reputation and safety. I had a friend I could count on.

We sometimes use the word "tough" as a negative to say someone is mean. That's not our definition here. We're talking about people who have strong convictions and aren't "driven and tossed by the winds" of people's opinions. Some people are like chameleons: They change their moods, words, and actions to please the person in front of them. When the people change, so do they. Others are critical and sarcastic. They may be smiling, but venom drips off their fangs. They're trying to cover up their insecurities by putting others down. And some people are so needy they suck the life out of everyone they know. They sound pitiful when convincing people to help them, to take care of them, and give them what they want. People may feel compassion at first—until they realize they're being played. But we (Rodney and Michelle) have had the pleasure of being friends with people who exhibit quiet confidence. They know who they are, and they're secure. In their relationships, they can give as well as take. They have developed (and are continuing to develop) convictions about what's most important to them. But they realize everything isn't a big deal, so they can let some things slide. Only a few things are hills worth dying on, and they're willing to go there because they're convinced those things are of ultimate importance.

People who model this kind of toughness stand their ground in hard times. After the Babylonians conquered God's people and their best and brightest young men were sent into exile to serve the king, the Babylonian court made demands on them. Daniel and his three friends were in this group. Part of the training was to give the young men a particular diet—one that didn't conform to Jewish dietary law. If they ate it, they would dishonor God, but if they didn't eat it, they could be killed. Before we go any further, think about their predicament: Their homeland had been devastated. It appeared that God had abandoned them to a cruel fate, and they were hundreds of miles from home, with no prospect of ever getting back. Their captors were demanding compliance, and they'd already seen how they dealt with resistance! It would have been very easy to buckle under the disappointment and pressure, but Daniel didn't do that: "Daniel purposed in his heart that he would not defile himself with the portion of the king's delicacies, nor with the wine which he drank; therefore he requested of the chief of the eunuchs that he might not defile himself" (Daniel 1:8, NKJV).

Daniel's character had won the admiration of the chief steward, so the door was open for Daniel to make him an offer. He and his friends would eat only vegetables and drink water for ten days. After that, if they appeared strong and healthy, the steward wouldn't demand they eat the training meals:

> *And at the end of ten days their features appeared better and fatter in flesh than all the young men who ate the portion of the king's delicacies. Thus the steward took away their portion of delicacies and the wine that they were to drink, and gave them vegetables.*
> —Daniel 1:15-16 (NKJV)

These four friends took a big risk to trust God to make them strong while eating only vegetables while others enjoyed steaks. It took courage. It took conviction. They were as tough as nails.

The rest of the story is that their conviction about food gave them courage to face any obstacle and demand. We've already seen how three of them trusted God in the face of seemingly certain death when the king threw them into the furnace. I don't think they would have had the strength to be strong then if they hadn't trusted God together earlier about the food and drink. Courage stimulates courage in those around us, and toughness is an example for others to follow.

But toughness doesn't always come out in fierce determination. We also need friends who encourage us to be strong enough to be tender. The apostle Paul was one of the toughest leaders the world has ever known. He suffered ridicule and beatings, shipwrecks and stoning, and homelessness and hunger. All of this could have made him cynical, but instead, he appreciated God's love more than ever. If we're strong in grace, we'll be kind to others—especially those who are hard to love. Paul explained it this way:

> *Since God chose you to be the holy people he loves, you must clothe yourselves with tenderhearted mercy, kindness, humility, gentleness, and patience. Make allowance for each other's faults, and forgive anyone who offends you. Remember, the Lord forgave you, so you must forgive others. Above all, clothe yourselves with love, which binds us all together in perfect harmony.*
> —*Colossians 3:12-14 (NLT)*

We can't love the unlovely and show God's kindness to those who want to hurt us unless we possess incredible inner strength—unless we're tough like Paul and Daniel and his friends.

Are we the kind of friends who have strong convictions and an unshakable security in the love of God? If we are, we'll attract people who either have that same strength or are in the process of developing it. These are the kinds of friendships that give us incredible ballast when the seas are rough, and these are the kinds of friendships that launch us to make a difference in the world.

> *When someone speaks truth into your life, you either get mad or you get mature.*
> —Lisa Young[76]

LOYAL

When my (Rodney's) niece Gabby became a freshman in high school, she had an anchor of a lifelong best friend. I'll call her Suzanne. The two had known each other for years and seemed to be joined at the hip. Both of the girls tried out for the cheerleading team, and both made the cut. But soon after school started, Suzanne became friends with another girl, Marcia. Gabby was happy to have another good friend, but that's not how Suzanne saw things. She became emotionally attached to Marcia, and together, they formed a secret alliance against Gabby. Relational triangles are usually awkward and painful, and this one was no exception. At one point, Gabby realized the other two girls were lying to her and about her. She was deeply hurt. She realized that loyalty kept is beautiful, but loyalty betrayed is devastating.

Life has a way of pulling people apart, causing little annoyances that turn into major disruptions in our most important relationships. But true friends fight through the misunderstandings and competing goals to be true to one another at all costs. Friends are loyal.

The story of David and Jonathan is one of the most beautiful in the Scriptures. Jonathan was King Saul's son, the presumptive heir to the throne. Their relationship begins after David's stunning defeat of the giant Goliath. The army of Saul was terrified of Goliath, and for weeks, they cowered behind their lines as they heard his taunts. David's father asked him to take bread and cheese to his brothers in the army, and when he arrived, he heard Goliath laugh at God's pitiful army. If nobody else would take on the giant, he would! He marched down into the valley

---

76 Lisa Young, *The Marriage You've Always Wanted* (Nashville, TN: Thomas Nelson, 2009), 142.

armed with only a sling and some rocks. His aim was true, and the giant fell down dead.

When David went to the king to give his report, Jonathan was there. Undoubtedly, he had been one of the amazed audience of soldiers on that day in the valley, and now he saw David, the shepherd boy, up close. The historian Samuel tells us,

> *By the time David had finished reporting to Saul, Jonathan was deeply impressed with David—an immediate bond was forged between them. He became totally committed to David. From that point on he would be David's number-one advocate and friend.*
>
> *Saul received David into his own household that day, no more to return to the home of his father.*
>
> *Jonathan, out of his deep love for David, made a covenant with him. He formalized it with solemn gifts: his own royal robe and weapons—armor, sword, bow, and belt. —1 Samuel 18:1-4 (MSG)*

The tables turned quickly in David's relationship with Saul. The king was jealous—and furious—when he heard people singing, dancing, and giving credit to David for the defeat of the Philistines at his expense. He was so insulted that the next day he tried to kill David with a spear ... twice! Saul made life miserable for the hero of the nation. He lied to David, cheated him out of a wife he had promised, and tried to capture him and kill him. This, of course, put Jonathan in quite a bind. David had every reason to assume his friend would choose his father's side, and he gave him an opportunity to bow out of the friendship. But Jonathan was loyal to David. In fact, Jonathan became a spy for David. He found out his father's plans to capture David, and he gave him the information. When David fled, Saul asked Jonathan why David wasn't eating dinner with them. Jonathan stretched the truth in his reply, and his loyalty to David was costly.

> *Saul exploded in anger at Jonathan: "You son of a slut! Don't you think I know that you're in cahoots with the son of Jesse, disgracing*

both you and your mother? For as long as the son of Jesse is walking around free on this earth, your future in this kingdom is at risk. Now go get him. Bring him here. From this moment, he's as good as dead!" —1 Samuel 20:30-31 (MSG)

Jonathan refused to give up David to his father. Later, in a great battle, both Saul and Jonathan were killed by the Philistines. David now became king. It was customary for a new king to kill all the descendants of the prior royalty, but David found Jonathan's son Mephibosheth, who was crippled, and showed extraordinary kindness by bringing him to live in the palace and eat at David's table every day.

For these two men, loyalty worked both ways. Loyalty is measured in the cost of remaining true to someone even when it's inconvenient, when others disagree, and when we lose something valuable. Jonathan was loyal to David at great expense, and David poured kindness on Jonathan's son to fulfill his covenant of love with his friend.

Loyalty says, "No matter what, you can count on me." A true friend celebrates our successes and grieves our losses. That's rare. It's much more common for people we know to be jealous about our successes and do what they can to cut us down to size, and begrudgingly acknowledge our losses but not enter into our pain.

> *Conflict always reveals character. How you respond shows who you really are!*
> —Rodney and Michelle Gage

COMMITTED

Loyalty is the inclination of the heart; commitment leads to actions that reflect this loyalty. True friends show their commitment in acceptance and alignment.

When we accept one another, we have a wonderful blend of grace and truth. We don't just roll over when we see our friend making a dumb decision or having a bad attitude. We love enough to step in and say what needs to be said. This means we say it in the way the friend can hear it, not to "get it off our chests" but to "put it in their hearts." We speak with grace because we've experienced grace. How did Jesus accept the disciples? By inviting them to join Him, overlooking most of their failures and flaws, gently correcting them when necessary, and spending plenty of time with them so they'd experience the full measure of His love for them. That's how Jesus relates to us too—and it's the mark of commitment in friendships.

Two people who have nothing in common rarely form deep friendships. We need at least some level of alignment of purpose if we're going to be friends. We share similar convictions about what's important and what's trivial, what God wants to do in and through us, and which hill we're willing to die on. In fact, the close bonds soldiers experience in combat are formed by exactly this kind of alignment—they're literally willing to die on the same hill for each other.

The story of Ruth is a beautiful tale of alignment. Naomi was her mother-in-law. Ruth was a Moabite woman who was an outcast to the Jews, but she had married Naomi's son. The women walked back to Palestine because life was unlivable in Moab. Both of their husbands had died, and they were destitute. As they approached the city of Bethlehem, Naomi had second thoughts. She told Ruth to go back home where she'd feel more comfortable among her own people, but Ruth had other ideas.

> *Ruth replied, "Don't ask me to leave you and turn back. Wherever you go, I will go; wherever you live, I will live. Your people will be my people, and your God will be my God. Wherever you die, I will die, and there I will be buried. May the L*ORD *punish me severely if I allow anything but death to separate us!" —Ruth 1:16-17 (NLT)*

In the Naomi's hour of despair, Ruth proved to be much more than a daughter-in-law—she was a committed friend who aligned the direction and future of her life with Naomi's. How strong was her commitment? As strong as death.

If you're going to make the shift in your personal life and marriage, and if your kids are going to thrive in today's culture, you need to learn to walk with the wise. Doing so is critical to achieving your destiny as a family. Finding friends who are tough will make you bolder and better. Friends who are loyal will be confidants to you and will celebrate you. Friends who are committed will accept you unconditionally and will be in alignment with your mission, vision, and values. They will affirm your goals and passions and walk through your struggles with you.

You might be asking, "How in the world do I find those kinds of people? And do those type of kids exist in elementary, middle, and high school for my children?" The answer is yes! However, we must be that kind of friend in order to have those kinds of friends. Again, you attract who you are. A great exercise for you to work through for yourself, as a couple, and with your kids is to identify the personality traits, characteristics, and qualities you would want to have in a friend. Be very specific. Once you identify those characteristics and qualities, ask yourself, *Am I that kind of person*? As we help our kids think about their friendships and their future mates, it's important to teach and reinforce to them that in order to have the right kinds of friends, we must first be the right kind of friend. Marriage is not about finding the right mate, it's about being the right mate. Before we move on to the fifth and final step of our 5-Step Plan of living with greater intention as a family, let's commit to making the necessary shifts in our current friendships and ask God to bring wise friends into our lives—friends who are tough, loyal, and committed who will help us live with greater intention.

THINK ABOUT IT:

1) How does this chapter define the quality of being a friend who is tough?
2) Why is tenderness also related to toughness?

3) Describe a friendship in which you were loyal when the other person was going through hard times. How did it affect him or her? How did the experience affect you?
4) Why is the courage to speak the truth in a winsome way an important part of accepting someone?
5) At this point in your life, who are a few people whose purpose and drive are closely aligned with yours? What are some ways you inspire and encourage each other?

DO IT:

Answer and discuss these questions as a family:
1) In relaxed times with your children, consider asking them questions about their friends. Make these appropriate for their age. Don't rush through this. One good question can launch wonderful conversations.

   Tell them about your friends when you were their age. Be honest, but appropriate.
   - Who would you say are my best friends? What do you see in our relationship?
   - Who are the people in your school (or youth group) who make you feel good about yourself? Tell me about that.
   - Who are the people in your class that you admire? What do you appreciate about them?
   - How does it affect you when people lie to you?
   - Who has been your best friend so far? What makes this person special to you?
   - Who are some people you don't trust? What's that about? (Be careful to avoid sharing names or too much information.)
   - Do you want my feedback about what I see in your friends? (If not, I may still give it when I think it's necessary!)

STEP 5

TEACH BY EXAMPLE

A SHIFT IN PURPOSE

CHAPTER 12

WHO'S ON POINT?

LEAD INTENTIONALLY

A leader is one who knows the way, goes the way, and shows the way.
—John C. Maxwell[77]

Tom Brady is generally considered the GOAT at the quarterback position—the greatest of all time. It didn't start that way. He started as quarterback for only two seasons at the University of Michigan. He wanted to play in the NFL, but he was drafted only in the sixth round in 2000, the 199th pick—a place from which very few players, much less quarterbacks, rise to become stars in the league. Brady proved to have all the skills, but even more, the mental tenacity to win. By the time he retired, he'd played in ten Super Bowls and won seven of them.

One of his Super Bowl losses came in 2018 when the Philadelphia Eagles beat them by a score of 41 to 33. That year, Brady had set a new record for the most passing yards in the postseason. With two minutes

---
[77] John C. Maxwell, *The 21 Irrefutable Laws of Leadership*, 135.

to play in the game, the Eagles had a five-point lead, and history suggested that Brady would pull out another stunning last-minute victory. But when he dropped back to pass, he was sacked and fumbled. The Eagles recovered, kicked a field goal to push the lead to eight points, and won the game.

When Brady got home, his children were taking the loss as hard as any Patriots fan. Brady recalls, "Benny was crying, Vivi was crying, and they were sad for me and sad for the Patriots." He saw this as a valuable moment in his children's lives: "But I just said to them, 'Look, this is a great lesson. We don't always win. We try our best, and sometimes, it doesn't go the way we want.'"[78]

Failure doesn't have to be the end of a dream. It may make us more determined, smarter, and with a clearer understanding of what it takes to succeed. In a *Business Insider* article about Brady's example to his kids, Abby Jackson points to *Shark Tank* investor Barbara Corcoran, who says she likes to invest in people from economically disadvantaged backgrounds. Corcoran asserts, "My bias toward the poor person coming up is they're usually hungrier. They're more injured. They have more to prove. So they've had a few bumpy endings, and they're used to failure, and, my God, what's more important in building a business than failing?"[79]

Tom Brady would likely agree. Losing stinks, but if we learn the lessons it can teach, it becomes the aroma of fertile soil for growth. This perspective is one of the most important ones we can pass to our children.

Remember this: *Your children will become who you are, so be who you want them to be.* This means we lead our families intentionally—not passively and just hoping things will turn out well but with an eye on the prize of growth in their character. This commitment requires us to shift and keep

---

78 Mike Reiss, "Tom Brady Says Super Bowl Loss Was Chance to Teach His Kids Lesson," *ESPN*, March 7, 2018, https://www.espn.com/nfl/story/_/id/22677136/tom-brady-says-super-bowl-loss-was-chance-teach-kids-lesson.

79 Abby Jackson, "Tom Brady used his Super Bowl loss to teach his kids an important lesson about failure," *Business Insider*, March 7, 2018, https://www.businessinsider.com/tom-brady-parenting-after-super-bowl-loss-2018-3.

shifting to continually reinforce the mission, vision, and values we want to instill in our children.

We've looked at the concept of imprinting and the work of bird experts wearing whooping crane costumes to raise chicks. The principle doesn't just work with birds; we see it in relationships between parents and children too. Most experts state that young animals, like chicks or our children, get their security and identity by watching parents and emulating them. In other words, our children absorb our attitudes and values almost effortlessly—for them anyway. As they watch, imprinting happens naturally, normally, and necessarily. It happens *naturally* because that's the way God made the parent-child relationship, it happens *normally* in the everyday events of life, and it happens *necessarily* because our kids desperately need good values to become healthy, productive adults. The flip side, of course, is that passive parents don't do enough to instill these values, and harsh parents instill counterproductive values that have an impact on children for the rest of their lives.

Of course, this doesn't mean that we automatically become exactly like our parents. Some of us become carbon copies of one or both of them, but many of us react and become the opposite. For instance, one might expect a harsh, condemning father to have a son who is just like him, but it's very likely he may produce a son who is gentle, compliant, and lives to please the people around him. Both the angry person and the kind person feel equally insecure, but they try to protect themselves and find meaning in very different ways.

All of us imprinted on our parents, and our kids are imprinting on us. The good news is that the values and behaviors we pick up as children can be changed.

> *We can't become who we need to be by remaining who we are.*
> —Rodney and Michelle Gage

GOD AS OUR MODEL

Jesus didn't just show up at a few events to teach and heal the sick. He spent over three years, day and night, with His closest followers. They saw Him interact with the religious leaders who ridiculed Him, and they saw Him tenderly touch lepers, people who were possessed by demons, the blind, and the sick. To be sure, His disciples were pretty slow on the uptake, but they eventually absorbed Jesus's heart and values. But we're not living in first-century Palestine, and we can't hang out with Jesus. Is it possible for us to have Him imprinted on our lives? Absolutely. In Paul's letter to the Ephesians, he makes the connection between God's heart and ours:

> *Get rid of all bitterness, rage, anger, harsh words, and slander, as well as all types of evil behavior. Instead, be kind to each other, tenderhearted, forgiving one another, just as God through Christ has forgiven you.*
>
> *Imitate God, therefore, in everything you do, because you are his dear children. Live a life filled with love, following the example of Christ. He loved us and offered himself as a sacrifice for us, a pleasing aroma to God. —Ephesians 4:31-33; 5:1-2 (NLT)*

As we imitate God, we'll realize we have very ungodly things in our hearts—bitterness, rage, anger, and so on. When we experience God's forgiveness for our sins, we're capable and motivated to forgive those who offend us. And we'll go beyond forgiving them to actually loving them, like Jesus, even when they don't love us in return. This doesn't mean we should become vulnerable to abusers. Those who are in a dangerous relationship (physically or emotionally) should protect themselves, but as they increasingly experience God's forgiveness and love, they won't hate the abuser any longer.

In this part of his letter, Paul uses the metaphor of changing clothes to illustrate the choices we make each day. We "put off" lying, stealing, harsh speech, and other sins, and we "put on" kindness, love, and honesty.

These are the choices you and I make all day, every day ... and our children are watching.

In another letter, Paul asks people to imprint on him as he follows Jesus. The letter to the Philippians is a thank you note for their help in his ministry. They had seen him cast a demon out of a young girl, preach, be thrown in prison, and rescued by an earthquake sent by God. He had impressed them, for sure! Now he tells them:

> *And now, dear brothers and sisters, one final thing. Fix your thoughts on what is true, and honorable, and right, and pure, and lovely, and admirable. Think about things that are excellent and worthy of praise. Keep putting into practice all you learned and received from me—everything you heard from me and saw me doing. Then the God of peace will be with you. —Philippians 4:8-9 (NLT)*

Paul says, "Watch me. Learn what I've learned. Believe what I believe. Do what I do ... and the God of peace will be with you." Is it presumptuous to ask our kids to follow us like that? No, because they're already doing it! The more poignant questions for us as parents are, what do they hear *in our talk*? And what do they see *in our walk*?

> *You teach what you know; you reproduce who you are.*
> —Jack Frost[80]

IN OUR TALK

We may think our children aren't listening when we're talking to our spouse in the car as the children ride in the back seat, but they hear more than we imagine. Experts tell us that only seven percent of communication is done in words; the rest is the tone of voice and gestures. So even if our actual words aren't poisonous, we can have a very negative impact on those listening by the way we say them.

---
80 Jack Frost, *Spiritual Slavery to Spiritual Sonship* (Shippensburg, PA: Destiny Image, 2002), 92.

A friend of ours said that when his son was about eight years old, the boy was riding his bike near him and hit a bump in the pavement. Instantly, the boy muttered, "Damn!"

His dad was surprised. He asked, "Where did you hear that word?"

The reply was immediate and crushing: "From you."

In Paul's letter to the Ephesians, he tells us to change clothes in our words: "Don't use foul or abusive language. Let everything you say be good and helpful, so that your words will be an encouragement to those who hear them" (Ephesians 4:29, NLT). That's a high standard, but it's how we correct our communication to be sweet, positive, and encouraging for those who are listening to us. This doesn't mean we can't say hard things to correct people, but we'll say them with kindness and hope, not to punish or manipulate.

IN OUR WALK

We're convinced that very little escapes the notice of children. They may not understand how to interpret every event, but they're watching every moment. What do they see? They're especially interested when they see:

- **How we respond to failure:** Do they see us blame someone else, deny the event even happened, minimize it by saying, "It's no big deal," or excuse ourselves, "I couldn't help it"? Or do they see us take responsibility, admit our part in the failure, and find the seed of growth to nurture for the future?
- **What matters to us:** We can say that God is most important to us or that our family is our priority, but is that what our kids see in action? Too often, the priorities we impart are our thirst for success, power, pleasure, and approval. If these are the things we talk most about—the things that make our eyes light up and our voices become more intense, and what we complain about when they don't happen—our behavior has sent a loud and clear message to our kids.

- **How we relate to our spouse:** We've heard it said that the best gift we can give our kids is for men to love their wives. It's also true that a great gift to children is for wives to respect their husbands . . . and for both to show it often and well. In broken homes, exes are tempted to disparage the former partner. Their deep hurt and resentment spill out and make a powerful impression on the kids. Be careful to communicate at least some degree of respect for one another, unless, of course, you need a restraining order or some other means of protecting you and your children.
- **How we spend our money:** Few choices have as much impact on our kids as how we use money. Does the desire for more control us, or are we content with what we have? Have we spent beyond our means and are drowning in debt so that we worry about it constantly? Or are we wise, careful in our spending, and joyful in our generosity? A friend told us that his mother constantly worried about money. Her father grew up in very hard times, so no matter how much money she had in the bank, she learned from him that it's never enough. Is that what we want our kids to pick up from us? Finding contentment in small things, spending time together doing free things, and teaching our kids good financial lessons will impart the right message to them concerning finances.
- **How we invest our time:** Time is a precious commodity that can be invested or wasted. Today, electronic devices have been almost implanted in our hands and in our ears, and the lives of many of us are dominated by screen time. There's nothing wrong with using the latest tools to learn and communicate—unless they consume our time. We're wise to evaluate how much time we're spending in activities that interfere with good communication with one another. We probably need to make some hard decisions about phones, computers, tablets, and the television. Change will probably be hard,

especially for those who are most invested in these devices, but soon the benefits of knowing each other will be obvious.

After Richard graduated from college with a degree in mechanical engineering, he took a job with one of the major oil companies. He worked at a plant in Texas for several years to learn the ropes. He and Alicia had gotten married when they were in college, and within a few years, they had a son and a daughter. Richard and some of those who graduated with him realized there was a proven path to promotions in the company. They met people who had been assigned to jobs all over the nation and in foreign countries. The track to success and the big salaries was being open to relocation, but Richard had other ideas about what gives meaning to success. He was offered promotions again and again, but he only took the ones that allowed his family to stay where they were. Others climbed much higher and made a lot more money, but Richard had done the cost-benefit analysis and concluded that his family was more important than those things. He was radically committed to avoiding drift in his family's relationships. Today, he's retired from the oil company. He looks back on all the decisions he made. He feels a little sad when he hears from former colleagues about their homes in the mountains or the beach—but not *that* sad. He looks at the life he provided for his son and daughter, who now have families of their own, and he's very grateful he had the good sense to choose his family over his career. He invested his time and his heart where they matter most.

> *What you put first will be what you are at the last.*
> —Brian Houston[81]

CONNECTING WITH GOD'S FAMILY

A few decades ago, a "regular church attender" came almost every Sunday out of the year. In recent years, a regular church attender was identified

---
81 Brian Houston, *Live Love Lead: Your Best Is Yet to Come!* (Grand Rapids, MI: Zondervan, 2015), 92.

as those who came three out of four Sundays a month, and, shockingly, today, regular attendance is defined as those who show up once or twice a month. The trend is clear. The problem isn't filling seats; it's about what we value, what we pursue, what we sacrifice, and what our choices are saying to our kids.

A study by LifeWay Research Group uncovered the impact of parents on their children's spiritual development:

- When both parents attend Bible study in addition to the Sunday service, 72% of their children attend Sunday school when grown.
- When only the father attends Sunday school, 55% of the children attend when grown.
- When only the mother attends Sunday school, 15% of the children attend when grown.
- When neither parent attends Sunday school, only 6% of the children attend when grown.
- The impact of fathers is especially profound. When a young person becomes a Christian, there's only a 3.5 percent probability that the rest of the family will trust in Christ. If the mother is the first to believe in Jesus, there's a seventeen percent probability that the rest will follow. But when the father is the first to believe, there is a 93 percent probability the rest of the family will follow Christ.[82]

As pastors for nearly thirty years, here is what we (Rodney and Michelle) know to be true—parents who treat the church as optional shouldn't be surprised when their children treat Jesus as unnecessary.

One of the main complaints of young people is that the adults they see in church live double lives—and quite often, they're talking about their parents. They see the adults sing worship songs on Sunday but are devoid of kindness, love, and honesty the rest of the week. We make a big mistake if we tell them they're wrong. Defensiveness only affirms their perceptions

---

[82] Nick Cady, "The Impact on Kids of Dad's Faith and Church Attendance," *Theology for the People*, June 20, 2016, https://nickcady.org/2016/06/20/the-impact-on-kids-of-dads-faith-and-church-attendance/.

and drives them further away. Instead, we need to invite dialogue and let them give us their perceptions without defying them, correcting them, or interrupting them. In fact, we need to learn those powerful and rare words that are too seldom used in tense conversations: "Tell me more of what you're thinking." And then we need to keep listening.

We can be honest about the disconnect on the part of many people. In fact, to some extent, all of us are hypocrites because we don't live up to the standards of true godliness. But our kids aren't looking for perfection. They're looking for honesty. If we can find the courage to admit when our actions don't match our stated beliefs, we'll open doors of meaningful communication that can last for the rest of our lives.

Encourage them to ask any question and share every opinion. They may push back on some of the basics of the faith. Don't overreact! Keep your composure and say, "Tell me more." Don't think that you have to get them to the "right answer" in the first conversation ... or in any conversation. If your kids are thinking, they'll explore the foundations of what they believe. It's part of growing up, not a character flaw. In fact, if a growing adolescent never voices concerns or questions about the important things in life, we should be worried!

YOUR TURN

In this book, we've explored the importance of establishing a personal and family mission (Why do we exist?), crafting a set of values (What do we care about?), and identifying the vision (Where are we going?). Now it's time to consider the strategy—How will we get there? You'll need a plan, and you'll need to refine the plan from time to time. The plan is about putting your intentions on paper so they're crystal clear and you know the process to reach your goals.

A company CEO can write these elements with the input of the management team or board, and parents (including single parents) have a similar privilege and responsibility of leading the family to articulate a plan to achieve the common goals. We suggest taking about thirty days to work through identifying what your mission, vision, and values will be as a family. It may take longer, and that's perfectly okay. The time spent isn't important; the quality of how you spend that time is. You can follow the shift acronym to guide your conversations. Start with the end in mind. Discuss who you want to become as a family. Paint a verbal picture of what you're striving for. Start with open-ended questions that allow everyone to articulate what their ideal family would look like. Discuss the specific purpose your family is going to fulfill. Allow that purpose to define your mission. Choose your non-negotiables. What will be important to you, and how are you going to behave as a family? If age appropriate, have everyone work through the Family Goal Tree discussed in chapter 7 and brainstorm ways you can work together and hold one another accountable to achieve those goals. Again, depending on the age and stage of each family member, you can take as much time as necessary so that everyone sees the benefit and value of working through these critical steps for long-term success as a family. This should be something the family sees as a blessing and benefit rather than a burden. The goal is to make this a fun and memorable experience.

When our girls were in middle school and Luke was in elementary school, we had our first family conversation about our mission, vision, and values. They were old enough to offer their opinions, and they were thrilled that we valued their input. We didn't use words that sounded like they came from corporate boardrooms. Instead, we used terms they easily understood and were memorable. The process of articulating these concepts together gave our family a strong sense of identity and ownership. We defined what we wanted to be known for. I (Michelle) found a decal at Hobby Lobby that perfectly describes our mission and vision as a family. It had a beautiful script font with the scripture verse found in Joshua 24:15: "But as for me and my family, we will serve the Lord." We wanted everyone who walked in and out of our home, including ourselves, to be reminded of our mission and vision as a family. We realized how each of us uniquely contributes to the success of the others, and together, we had a sense of destiny.

As you talk to your family, share your convictions about what's most important to you, and invite the input of everyone in the family. Take the long view—don't expect quick, simple answers to life's most significant issues. Encourage dialogue, study, talk some more, and have deeper conversations. Sooner or later, you'll have a plan to pursue what matters most, how you relate to each other, how you spend your money, and how you invest your time.

This is where the proverbial "rubber meets the road." A few of us are instinctive and don't seem to need much planning, but the rest of us need a clear, compelling plan that captures our hearts and gives us clear tracks to run on. Create a plan that works for you and your family. Have a blend of tenacity and flexibility, and realize that each person in your family may need something different to keep them motivated. Some need structure, some need room for creativity, and some need more encouragement than others. Be a student of your family. Take the time to craft this plan, and watch how God uses you to inspire the people you love.

THINK ABOUT IT:

1) What values, attitudes, and behaviors did you absorb from your parents?
2) Did you copy them or react in an opposite way? Explain your answer.
3) What do your children hear, and what do they pick up in nonverbal cues when they hear you talk? How do you know?
4) How are you modeling a response to failure?
5) Are you modeling the values that matter most to you?
6) What do your kids see in your relationship with your spouse (or your ex)?

7) If your kids follow your example about time and money, where will it lead them?
8) What can you do to let them see an authentic relationship with God and with God's people in the church?

DO IT:

Answer and discuss these questions as a family:
1) With your spouse, take some time to think, pray, and plan your strategy to intentionally implement the changes you've identified from previous chapters and lessons learned here.
2) Share your plans with your children. Value their questions and engage them in conversations about how your family will live out your values.

CHAPTER 13

THE POWER OF UNCONDITIONAL LOVE

EXTEND FORGIVENESS AND MERCY MORE CONSISTENTLY

The best use of life is love. The best expression of love is time. The best time to love is now.
—Rick Warren[83]

I (Rodney) would like to say I'm the paragon of virtue when it comes to responding to my children's misbehavior through the years with calm and wisdom, but I'm still on the learning curve. I think I did pretty well with my daughters, Becca and Ashlyn, but with Luke, as he grew

---
83 Rick Warren, *The Purpose Driven Life: What on Earth Am I Here For?* (Grand Rapids, MI: Zondervan, 2002), 125.

older, the testosterone levels from both of us kicked in. I'm afraid I went overboard sometimes. I learned that when I raised my voice, Luke raised his! Far too often, I respond by raising mine again, and he would follow my lead. The unspoken but very real question both of us were asking was, *Who's going to win this shouting match?* My assumption was that since I'm the dad, I should win. I learned that Luke didn't always make that assumption! As you can imagine, our "conversations" didn't turn out well. After several rounds of escalation, Luke would walk off and go to his room. We would both stew for a while—long enough for me to feel guilty for not having enough self-control and empathy. I would regret things I said and how I said them, but instead of letting the anger and guilt take root, I would take the steps toward Luke's room, knock on the door, and ask him to forgive me for losing it. I would always tell him that it was wrong of me to lose my cool, and I would always reassure him of my love for him. You would have to know Luke's personality to appreciate this, but every time, he would look at me, smile, and say, "Yeah, Dad. I know you love me." I'd walk away relieved that my relationship with my son was restored, but I often wondered how I let that eruption of anger happen . . . again . . . and again?

We're steeped in a culture that talks a lot about love but seldom understands it beyond a superficial level. In describing love between a man and a woman, the messages are all about hot romance and tender feelings. And in parents' relationships with their kids, it seems that love means giving them everything they can ever want. If we're not careful, we won't just drift—we'll be swept downstream in the culture's torrent! It helps if we start on or get on the right track when we try to understand the nature of love.

> *To love someone means to see him as God intended him to be.*
> —Fyodor Dostoevsky[84]

---

84 Fyodor Dostoevsky, *The Brothers Karamazov*, trans. Richard Pevear and Larissa Volokhonsky (New York, NY: Farrar, Straus and Giroux, 1990), 758.

CONSUMER OR COMMITTED?

There are two kinds of relationships: *consumer* relationships and *committed* relationships. The two are miles apart. Most of the connections we have are the consumer type. The question we inherently ask is, "What's best for me?" As long as the relationship meets our needs, we'll stay, but when something better comes along, we drop one and pick up the other. My (Michelle's) relationship with the salesperson at a clothing boutique is like this. If she can sell me a beautiful dress at a good price, I'll probably go back to buy another outfit from her . . . unless I see an ad from another store with a more enticing offer. Where we shop for clothes, groceries, fast food, internet services, and virtually every brick and mortar or online store are determined because one meets our needs better than another. In these cases, our needs are more important than the relationship.

That's all fine and reasonable when we're thinking about buying a cup of coffee, but it doesn't work in our most important relationships. If we have a consumer mentality in our marriage, when our spouse doesn't meet our needs, we think about bailing—maybe not the first time, but after a while, the unmet expectations take a toll. We could look at all the statistics about adultery, but studies also show a lot of people who fantasize about someone more attractive never actually act on their daydreams. But their daydreams are indications that their hearts aren't getting what they need now and are leaning toward getting their needs met by someone, sometime, and somehow.

We can also have a consumer relationship with our kids. When they excel in sports or make great grades in school, we feel proud because their success reflects our great parenting—or that's what we want others to conclude. But when they aren't too gifted in athletics, academics, choosing friends, or weight or complexion, we feel embarrassed. And we don't like feeling embarrassed! To solve the problem, we put pressure on our kids to perform better. We say it's for their sake so they'll excel later in life—and we're sure there's some of that motivation in the mix, but most of the pressure we put on our kids is because their performance and appearance aren't meeting our needs. No, we don't plan to ditch them and find other kids to bring home, but we sure wish they'd do a better job of reflecting our high standards of excellence!

A very different kind of relationship is a commitment, in which the relationship is more important than our needs. Instead of "what's best for me," here, people pursue what's best for the other person. We sacrifice for each other, not because we have to but because we cherish the other. Only a few relationships rise to this kind of commitment: marriage, parenting our children, with God, and our spiritual family.

Another way to describe these strong, unbending relationships is as a "covenant." Throughout the Bible, God makes covenants with people, from Adam to Noah to Abraham to Moses to the new covenant in Jesus. Some of these are conditional. God says, "I'll do this, but you have to do that." But some are unconditional. God says, "I'll never leave you or forsake you." The conditional ones use a stick to get our attention and compel compliance, but the unconditional ones warm our hearts and inspire us to follow the One who has proclaimed His love for us. In our marriages and as we parent our children, our understanding of these covenant relationships gives us a firm foundation to love unconditionally. We've experienced the love, forgiveness, and acceptance of God, so we pour out love, forgiveness and acceptance to the ones we love—even when it's inconvenient, even when they aren't meeting our needs, and even when they don't appreciate what we do for them.

THE DIFFERENCE

Men and women seem to speak different languages, and some have said they're from different planets! In Paul's letter to the Ephesians, he describes the deep commitment husbands and wives have for each other. The relationship isn't for convenience, or even for thrills. Instead, it's a picture of our relationship with God. He tells husbands to love their wives "just as Christ loved the church" and "gave up his life" in sacrificial love. But he gives a different instruction to wives: to respect their husbands (See Ephesians 5:21-33).

Dr. Emerson Eggerichs studied married couples and discovered a fascinating fact in his research:

We believe love best motivates a woman and respect most powerfully motivates a man. Research reveals that during marital conflict a husband most often reacts unlovingly when feeling disrespected, and a wife reacts disrespectfully when feeling unloved. We asked 7,000 people the question, "When you are in a conflict with your spouse or significant other, do you feel unloved or disrespected?" 83% of the men said "disrespected" and 72% of the women said "unloved." Though we all need love and respect equally, the felt need differs during conflict, and this difference is as different as pink is from blue![85]

It is wise for a husband to understand that the identity of his wife is tied to her work professionally as much as it is domestically as a wife and mother. Husbands can help their wives feel loved, supported, and appreciated by calling them during the day, offering to run errands, volunteering to change diapers or wash dishes, calling in dinner date reservations, and doing other things specific to their relationship. When men don't do things like this for their wives, the wives feel taken for granted and unappreciated. And each wife needs to realize her husband's identity is also, to a significant degree, tied up in his work, his intelligence, skills, and accomplishments. When she doesn't show confidence, give encouragement, and celebrate him, it crushes him . . . and he may react with sarcasm, anger, or silence. When wives feel adored and husbands feel honored, children have a safe place to grow and thrive. They see love in action in their parents' relationship, and they internalize the unique strength of a committed relationship. They may not be able to articulate

---

85 Dr. Emerson Eggerichs, "What Is Love and Respect," *Love and Respect*, https://loveandrespect.com/.

the difference between a consumer relationship and a committed one, but they instinctively know the difference.

This isn't an academic exercise for children. They're dramatically affected by the type of relationship they see in the home. They'll look for friends who treat them with honor and speak the truth, and they'll look for a spouse who has these values. Then they'll instill their children with the values of a committed relationship, and the legacy is passed from generation to generation.

> *Our children are not going to be just "our children"—they are going to be other people's husbands and wives and the parents of our grandchildren.*
> —Mary S. Calderone[86]

PAY IT FORWARD

We've had the privilege of watching a lot of amazing parents who have modeled love and respect to their kids. Here are some of the most important practices they've used:

Notice, Name, and Nurture Strengths

It's so easy for parents to become fixated on the misbehavior and flaws in our children that we find ourselves constantly correcting them. We need to become experts at finding the good and shining a spotlight on it in our kids. Notice their success, and even their progress toward success. Put a label on the strength they display so the word becomes a part of the child's identity, and then provide resources to help the child excel in that area.

A friend's son showed remarkable promise in art from the time he was only four or five years old. In fact, he began drawing in perspective when he was five. His dad, by his own admission, is artistically backward, and could have squashed his son's talents because he was uncomfortable with

---

[86] Mary S. Calderone, quoted in *Citatis*, https://citatis.com/a13529/1183c4/.

his son having a talent he didn't have himself. But, luckily, he quickly realized his son had a gift that needed to be developed. He bought his son plenty of art supplies, had great conversations with him about his drawings, and became his biggest cheerleader. Throughout his school years, the young man honed his talents. He majored in fine arts in college and today makes a good living as an illustrator.

Invest Time and Affection

Raising strong, confident children is as much art as it is a science, but two things are absolutely necessary: time and tenderness. Some have insisted that our kids need only "quality time," but in the experience of thousands of parents I know, the only way to have quality time is to have quantity time. Yes, we're busy. Yes, many of us work long hours. I'd say that we need to make sure our priorities are aligned with God's. If we have to work overtime for a season, that's no big deal, but if we've made our careers more important than our children, we will pay a steep price for it down the road—at the expense of being involved in our children's lives.

Meaningful touch is just one way to show affection to our kids, but it's one of the best. Even young men don't shake off a hug or a hand on their backs with a smile that says, "You mean the world to me!"

Be a Good Forgiver

Many of us aren't good at giving or receiving forgiveness. The best we can do is get to a point that we tolerate the person who has offended us, but that's certainly not the same thing as genuinely forgiving them. When someone wrongs us, they create a debt: they owe us. We can eliminate the debt in one of two ways—either we make them pay the debt or we pay it. If someone comes into our house and breaks a vase, either he will pay for another one, we'll buy a new one, or we'll do without one. In one way or another, someone will pay for it. In forgiveness, we're taking the step of paying the debt down ourselves. For small offenses, we can absorb the loss pretty quickly, but for abuse or betrayal, the process takes a while.

How do we know if we've forgiven someone who's hurt or wronged us? One of the surest ways is to analyze our thoughts about the person. Do we secretly (or not so secretly) delight when we hear she's having problems? Are we glad when we hear someone else talk about his faults? Do we daydream about her suffering for what she's done?

We can be good forgivers only to the extent of understanding how much God has forgiven us. Our debt was paid by Jesus—fully and for all time. The last words He spoke on the cross before He died were, "Paid in full." Out of a heart overflowing with the gratitude of being forgiven, we can forgive those who have hurt us.

Our children see revenge and retaliation every day at school. Do they see something else at home? Of course, this extends immediately to the way we respond to our kids when they disobey. We forgive them, and our love always wants the best for them, so as we forgive, we hold them accountable. In this, we give them correction without condemnation. We don't call them names, we don't snarl, we don't turn and walk away in disgust, and we don't continually call attention to the offense or wrong. Instead, we can say, "Son, I forgive you. Now, what will you do next time?" For some of us, this kind of response is easy because that's the way our parents treated us, but for many, this is a foreign language! We've never seen it, we've never known it was possible, and we're starting in the hole. But it's still possible even for those of us who are new to the experience of forgiveness. We can admit our tendency to carry a grudge, focus on the forgiveness Christ has given us in abundance, and practice saying, "I forgive you. What will you do next time?"

Incorporate the Three Cs: Be Calm, Be Clear, and Enforce Consequences

One of the main reasons that parents have conflicts with their kids is that they don't communicate clear expectations, and even when they do, they don't follow through on the consequences. This confuses children and makes them assume we don't really care. And when they make this assumption, we get angry and defensive . . . and more demanding. Ever been there? We (Rodney and Michelle) certainly have. Even when we're clear about our expectations, we can expect teenagers to push the boundaries.

When Becca was in high school, she developed a friendship with a boy in her class. We thought he was just one of the large group of friends she hung out with, but at one point we discovered they had moved past friendship to infatuation. She knew he wasn't on the "Approved for Dating" list (if there had been one), so she had tried to hide their relationship. Rodney and I (Michelle) were pretty upset.

The boy was very popular and charming . . . actually, too charming. When he showed interest in Becca, she was thrilled. He had a reputation of being a ladies' man—a fact that Becca either didn't know or ignored, but Rodney and I knew. When we told Becca that we didn't want her to be around him, she became furious. She accused us of overreacting and judging him unfairly. I explained that we knew of his reputation, and we didn't want her to get hurt. She stormed off to her room and slammed the door. Rodney called the boy to let him know that their relationship was over, and we didn't want him to pursue Becca anymore.

We loved Becca too much to let her stay in a relationship that would bring her misery. Of course, she insisted that we needed to trust her, but we remained firm in our assessment of the boy's character. Thankfully, over a few weeks, Becca realized what we'd said about the boy was true, and she understood why we had set such a hard boundary about their relationship. It proved to be a very positive experience for her because she realized her infatuation could have led to choices she would regret for the rest of her life.

> *Parenting is a delicate balance of convincing your child they can do anything in life while simultaneously screaming, "Don't Do That!" every three minutes.*
> —David Crank[87]

These three Cs are essential for good parenting, healthy relationships, and real growth in a child's character. First, be *calm*. Far too often, we interpret every disagreement or delay in our children's obedience as a personal offense. Whether they mean it this way or not, we need to refuse to light the fuse! Stay calm. Take a deep breath, maybe walk around for a few minutes, and when you're ready, come back to speak with self-control to your child (and anyone else within earshot).

Second, the expectations need to be very *clear* and age-appropriate: We don't set a curfew for a toddler. So, part of the art of parenting is to determine what is a reasonable expectation for children at each stage of development, including their room, household chores, homework, money, relationships, video games, particular sites that are off limits, and on and on. I would recommend that you don't give your child, at any age, a manual of all the demands of the household. They follow plenty of rules at school and may resent having even more rules at home. Expectations and restrictions should be shared out of love for your child for their safety and well-being—not out of being a gatekeeper. Keep it as simple and clear as possible. When these rules and expectations become habits, add another one or two.

Third, make sure the *consequences* are very clear, are reasonable, fit the offense, and are enforceable. If one day out of the blue you frustratingly say, "If you don't clean up your room, you'll be grounded and I'm taking

---
87 David Crank, *Live Your Dreams: Achieving Your Full Potential* (St. Louis, MO: Crank Ministries, 2017), 94.

your phone for a month," you'll likely lose credibility in two ways: You haven't matched the consequence with the offense, and you probably won't follow through with it anyway. This would only heighten frustrations all around. It's far better to have a dialogue with your children about the consequences, and even *let them determine* what sort of consequence is appropriate for their action or non-action. Quite often, they'll be stricter than you are, and you may need to ratchet them back a bit.

By all means, follow through with the consequences. You can adjust them next time if they're too light or too strong, but do what you promised you'd do—especially if the child has established the expectation and consequences.

Let's repeat: Through it all, be calm and kind. We're the grownups in the room, and we need to act like it. Yes, there are times when we want to scream . . . times when we're at the end of our ropes and we don't think we can take it anymore. In the PBS documentary, *Baseball*, Dick Stockton described the self-control of Pittsburgh Pirates slugger Willie Stargell in the 1975 World Series:

> *Willie Stargell really was a good man. All the hopes that he would direct toward other ballplayers came true in his case. I remember the 1971 World Series where those teams [the Baltimore Orioles and Pittsburgh Pirates], same two teams that played seven games, and Stargell was a great player that year, and the leader, had led the League in runs batted in and did almost nothing in the World Series. He popped, struck out—same in the Playoffs. And he never complained, he never said anything, he walked back, he never threw his bat down. And I went up to him after the series, and near the end, and I said, "How can you do this? You must be dying." And his little son, Wilver Jr., Wilver Stargell Jr. was playing in the locker and Willie made a gesture toward him and he said, "The time comes*

when a man really has to be a man." It just came out of him like that. And that's the kind of man he was.[88]

Willie Stargell could have thrown his bat, cursed, and stomped around the dugout or the clubhouse, but he realized the model he provided for his little son was more important than his baseball reputation. "The time comes when a man really has to be a man" . . . what an example we can lead with as parents!

KEEP FILLING THE TANK

Dr. Ross Campbell has a powerful illustration for parents. In *How to Really Love Your Child*, he says that it's our job to fill, and keep filling, the "emotional tank" in our kids:

> *This tank is figurative, of course, but nevertheless is real. Each child has certain emotional needs, and whether these emotional needs are met (through love, understanding, discipline, and so on) determines many things. First of all, it determines how a child feels: whether the child is content, angry, depressed, or joyful. Second, it affects behavior: whether the child is obedient, disobedient, whiny, perky, playful, or withdrawn. Naturally, the fuller the emotional tank, the ore positive feelings and the better the behavior.*[89]

Are we filling their tanks or depleting them? If they're in school, they probably come home many days with their emotional tanks bone dry. At every age, they need our love, our words of hope and affirmation, and our faith that they have a bright future. We fill their tanks with our words, our touch, our smiles, our confidence, and our time. When their tanks are low, we can step up and fill them—even when we're tired, even when we're busy, and even when we'd rather be somewhere else. That's what it means to love our children unconditionally. And you'll likely be surprised that when you share your love with your child, that your own emotional

---

88   Ken Burns, *Baseball*, 9th Inning, *PBS*, https://www.pbs.org/kenburns/baseball/.
89   Dr. Ross Campbell, *How to Really Love Your Child*, (Colorado Springs, CO: David C. Cook, 2015), 40.

tank starts to fill back up, too. The simple ways a child displays their love for you will certainly lift you up even on the most draining of days.

One of the very practical things my (Rodney's) father did for my brothers and me is that he made a point of introducing us to people he respected. They were prominent athletes, political leaders, or gifted speakers, and all of them had won my father's heart—usually because they had overcome incredible odds to achieve success. Meeting them filled my emotional tank because I felt included in my dad's world, and these people inspired me to dream bigger and reach higher. One summer he took me with him to serve as an intern. That was the first time I really understood what had captured his heart, what motivated him to sacrifice, and how he lived out his values. That summer propelled me to imagine how God might use me, too. I saw how God could use me in the lives of young people, and my sense of passion became much clearer and stronger. But it doesn't stop with me. Exposing our three children to outstanding people is one of the ways Michelle and I are trying to fill their emotional tanks and lift them higher. One summer, my dad invited me to serve as an intern in his outreach events held in different cities across the country. That was the first time I really understood and learned to appreciate my father's ministry, where God used him to affect so many people's lives. That summer propelled me to imagine how God might use me too. I saw how God could use me in the lives of young people, and my sense of passion became much clearer and stronger. But it doesn't stop with me. Exposing our three children to outstanding people is one of the ways Michelle and I are trying to fill their emotional tanks and lift them higher. We always look for opportunities to introduce our kids to people who are making a difference and especially those who have overcome obstacles to get there. We always believed they would benefit from being around other great leaders and people of influence. We believed it would serve as fuel for their confidence and vision for their futures.

> *Vision can't be taught; it must be caught.*
> —Freddie Gage

As parents, we have to remember that one of the great responsibilities we have is to create an atmosphere in our home and to establish a relationship with our children that is like freshly poured cement. We only have a short amount of time with them before the cement hardens. Now is the time to make a lasting, positive impression on the wet cement of our children's hearts and lives before it's too late.

THINK ABOUT IT:

1) How would you describe the differences between a consumer relationship and a committed relationship?
2) How can you tell which kind you have in a marriage? With your children?
3) Why is it important to understand that, in general, wives thrive when they feel loved and husbands thrive when they feel respected?
4) What are your children's strengths? How can you affirm them and provide resources for them to excel in these areas?
5) Are you a good forgiver? Explain your answer. If you have work to do on forgiving others more completely, what do you need to be able to forgive from your heart?
6) After reading the section on setting expectations and enforcing consequences, do you need to make any changes with your kids? If so, describe your first steps.
7) What are some ways you can fill the emotional tanks of your children today? What difference will it make for your family?

DO IT:
Answer and discuss these questions as a family:
1) Make a list of people you admire, especially those who have overcome long odds.
2) Make an appointment to take at least one of your children to meet one of them, or have the person come to your house for dinner or just a conversation. After it, talk to your child about the courage the person displayed.

CHAPTER 14

LEAVING THE NEST

RAISE THEM AND RELEASE THEM

Part of the thrill of guiding children into adulthood is the release. But it's also a parent's greatest act of surrender. Still, you have to let them go. Start now.
—Charles Swindoll[90]

In the years that we (Rodney and Michelle) have been family mentors, we've seen it all. Parents need to give their kids roots and wings. Roots keep them grounded in who they are, and wings to empower them to soar as they become who they are meant to be.

Sadly, not all parents provide these twin necessities. Some provide roots without wings. We've watched young people who have been smothered by well-meaning parents leave for college or their careers without the confidence or skills necessary for success. Their parents thought they were

---

90 Charles R. Swindoll, *The Strong Family: A Parenting Resource for Raising Children* (Nashville, TN: Thomas Nelson, 1997), 203.

helping by giving their kids everything they needed and making their decisions for them, but the result was that their children were more like toddlers than adults. They were impulsive or indecisive (sometimes at the same time), and were often confused because they hadn't developed the skills of analysis and decision-making. Sometimes, the parents want their grown children to remain dependent on them. I know parents who call their kids in college every day, and even worse, their kids feel the need to call home every day!

We've also seen some young adults struggle because their parents were physically or emotionally detached, and the kids had to figure things out on their own. Their parents gave them wings of independence but very shallow roots. Sometimes, the parents' preoccupation is due to something out of their control, like their own health crisis or critical problems with another person in the family, and their attention is absorbed by the drama. But some parents are so fixated on their own careers (or hobbies) that they essentially abandon their families emotionally. Without strong relationships at home, some of the young people became fiercely self-reliant, but some gravitated to anyone who would pay attention to them—sometimes with disastrous effects. No one loved them, no one believed in them, so they spend the rest of their lives searching for affection and meaning. When they marry and have kids, they don't have a clue about how to relate to them, and the cycle often continues.

> *Without roots, kids drift. Without wings, they won't shift.*
> —Rodney and Michelle Gage

But we've also watched wise parents build character and life skills into their children. They didn't wait until the day before their kids were leaving home. They began the process when they were very young, and over about eighteen years of teaching, training, modeling, and countless events of trial and error, their children gradually acquired what they needed to make a difference in the world, make hard decisions, and build strong relationships.

The goal of parenting isn't to make our kids permanently dependent on us; it's to give them what they need to be healthy, independent, creative, loving adults. Roots *and* wings. Psychologist Charleen Alderfer explains the importance of both:

> *A healthy family provides a secure environment for growth and learning. There is a sense of "we-ness" and belonging on the part of each member. There are fair limits that are understandable and discussable. There are boundaries that protect members and boundaries that expand to let in new members and new information. There is a sense of loyalty that is strong and does not impede one from developing into a person with individual ideas, dreams, and behavior. Humor in a family improves its general health and well-being. There is no question that the way a family functions will define, to a large measure, how well a child will develop.*
>
> *Roots—a knowledge of belonging, and wings—a recognition of the need for autonomy; these together are what children need from their families to become productive, well-functioning and happy adults.*[91]

BEGIN WITH THE END IN MIND

It's never too early to think, plan, and pray about launching our kids into their adult lives. If our goal is to give them security and confidence, we'll start when they're little to impart the concepts of independence. Actually, we're not alone in our goal. God has created us to separate—to *individuate*, to use a psychologist's term—from our parents. We see this most dramatically in two of the stages of development: about two years old and in adolescence. When children turn two, they begin to

---

[91] Charleen Alderfer, "Roots and Wings," *PsychCentral*, October 8, 2018, https://psychcentral.com/lib/roots-and-wings/.

find their own voice, their own desires, and their own possessions. They have been very dependent on their parents, especially their mothers, but now they pull away. They stomp their little feet and say, "No!" to every question or instruction. They didn't suddenly become demon-possessed! They're just taking the first steps toward finding their own identity apart from their parents.

Of course, the second stage of pulling away is adolescence. The combination of opportunities, peer pressure, and hormones has a powerful effect to drive teens to separate from their parents. For some, no matter what the parents think about any topic, the teenager disagrees. A few remain compliant, but most push the boundaries. They experiment with ideas, people, and goals. This isn't abnormal; it's completely normal. They're trying to establish themselves and figure out their place in the world.

Too often, parents interpret the pulling away during adolescence as a personal offense. Every disagreement is seen as a threat to what they hold dear and a blow to the values they've tried to instill in their kids. The teenager appears to be defiant and out of control . . . and, in fact, they may be defiant, but their attitude and behavior usually isn't as far out of bounds as the parents assume. To be honest, many parents make things far worse by reacting too strongly and taking everything personally. For many of us, it's a very important shift to reframe what's going on with our teenagers . . . and see it as completely normal. If we understand the importance of this stage, we'll be their biggest cheerleaders instead of being perceived as prison guards.

Actually, our children's behavior does reflect on us. This fact can have opposite effects: We can either try to control and manipulate them, or we can love them well so they'll want to listen to our advice. The psalmist gave this insight about parenting:

Children are God's love-gift; they are heaven's generous reward. Children born to a young couple will one day rise to protect and provide for their parents. Happy will be the couple who has many

of them! A household full of children will not bring shame on your name but victory when you face your enemies, for your offspring will have influence and honor to prevail on your behalf!
—Psalm 127:3-5 (TPT)

> *Let's leave our kids and grandkids more than just memories; let's leave them a legacy.*
> —Rodney and Michelle Gage

DEEPER ROOTS, BROADER WINGS

It's the job of teenagers to create an identity that's separate from their parents. We can either support them as they work this out, or we can resist and resent them. We'll offer a few suggestions:

Develop a Vision

At every stage of your child's development, use your imagination to envision how a son or daughter's personality and interests might translate into a successful adult. Point to people, famous or familiar, who live remarkable lives. All of us need heroes; talk about the people who inspire you, and notice the ones that make your child's eyes widen. As you develop a vision for your child's future, remain open and flexible. God may have other plans, and your child may develop other interests, but having a sense of hope will be infectious.

When Becca was in college, she got a full scholarship for her singing, and she loved it. During the summer after her junior year, she became an intern at a large church in Birmingham, Alabama, and her heart was tugged toward ministry. The church was affiliated with another college, and they offered her a full scholarship, too. Since she was born, Rodney and I have communicated that we believed God had something special for her (just like we've communicated vision and hope to Ashlyn and Luke). Now, Becca was torn between two incredible opportunities.

Rodney and I sat down with her and talked through the pros and cons of each path based on her deepest, clearest, most compelling sense of passion. After a lot of discussion and prayer, she decided to leave the school she had been attending and enroll in the college in Birmingham. We're really proud of her for many reasons, but certainly one of them is that she has a mature decision-making process. We knew that either way she chose, she had a bright future, and God had great plans for her, no matter what.

Preparation

The point of releasing children into the world, usually at about eighteen years old, requires preparation—of them and of us. One of our favorite quotes is by Zig Ziglar: "Success occurs when opportunity meets preparation."[92] For years, we guide, we equip, and we let them take more responsibility for their decisions so when the time comes, they feel excited and confident. A major part of preparing them for the future is letting them fail. Yes, we celebrate their successes, but we need to avoid protecting them too much from failure. When they were little, it was our responsibility to protect them because they were so vulnerable, but as they grow in their teen years, they need to develop wisdom, to choose friends wisely, and to make good decisions—and one thing is certain: They'll fail at these things from time to time. Their failure may hurt us worse than it hurts them, but if we're too protective, they won't learn from their mistakes, and they won't gain the wisdom they desperately need to navigate the world apart from home.

So . . . maybe we need to prepare ourselves as much as we prepare them. We need to be self-aware to know if *we're* making decisions *they* should be making and preventing them from learning the lessons that can only be learned from failure. If we realize we're "too"—too involved or too hands-off—we can adjust. Quite often, husbands and wives are on

---

[92] Attributed to Zig Ziglar, *See You at the Top*.

opposite ends of this stick. If they can avoid seeing each other as "wrong," they can moderate each other and find a good balance. A lot depends on their communication. In our observations, a lot of parents are on the same page as long as their kids are little. The fireworks happen as children grow in responsibility and independence, and the kids are caught in the middle. That's not good for anybody!

Do your homework. Read blogs and books about launching kids into adulthood. Talk to people who have been down this road and learned the necessary lessons. And realize each child is different: One may go through this period smoothly, but a sibling may struggle with the complexity of pulling away but still staying connected.

The Scriptures give a powerful analogy about the principle of sowing and reaping. Like a farmer who gets tired and maybe even discouraged with all the work it takes before he sees the first signs of harvest, parents can lose heart too. In his letter to the Galatians, Paul encouraged them, "And don't allow yourselves to be weary or disheartened in planting good seeds, for the season of reaping the wonderful harvest you've planted is coming!" (Galatians 6:9, TPT)

Encourage Like Crazy

People live for encouragement, and they die without it. Teenagers are especially vulnerable to self-doubt. Everything in their lives is up for grabs—relationships at home, friends, relationships with the opposite sex, powerful drives ignited by hormones, and an uncertain future, to name a few of their dilemmas. More than ever, they need us to look past their craziness (at least most of it) and give them what no one else on earth can give them: unconditional love.

As we saw in an earlier chapter, there are three messages all young people need to hear: "I love you," "I'm proud of you," and "You're really good at . . ." We can use a variety of words to communicate these encouragements. They matter because, believe it or not, teenagers still look to their parents for support. We're like mirrors. When they look at us, do our faces say something affirming, or do they say something critical? The words will be counterproductive if we don't mean it. When we're upset with them (and it'll happen; I guarantee it), we should take some deep breaths and recalibrate our hearts so we can mean it when we say, "Hey, don't forget. No matter what happens, I love you so much. And I want you to know that I'm really proud to be your mom (or dad)." Do you think that'll make a difference? Of course, it will.

Noticing and resourcing strengths will inspire and give a firm foundation for success. Teenagers, no matter how they look on the outside, are almost universally fragile on an emotional level. We can build confidence by describing how we can see their strengths having an impact on others. It's more than putting a label on their talents, which is important as a first step. We can provide much more encouragement as we see a bright future for them and describe it in some detail. Of course, a lot of pieces will be missing, and we won't be the ones to put those pieces in place, but a vision of the future seldom falls on deaf ears.

Guide Appropriately

This is where parenting teenagers gets tricky. How much do we try to guide our children, and how much do we let them take the reins? This isn't an easy question. The answer depends on a number of factors, such as the age and developmental stage of the child, personality and confidence, the level of our anxiety based on our own past mistakes, the opportunities, and the timing of decisions. The goal is to find a happy medium where you're not pushing and you're seen as an ally.

We (Rodney and Michelle) have taught our kids to trust God to open *and* close doors for them. They need to develop discernment to recognize the opportunities and obstacles, and just as important, the timing of their important decisions. One of the hardest things for any of us is waiting, so we've talked with Becca, Ashlyn, and Luke about the three answers to prayer. God may say "yes," He may say "no," and He may say "not now." The last one is often the most difficult to hear. God's delays aren't necessarily God's denials. In all of this, we realize it's important for them to make their own decisions. As they've matured, they've taken on more responsibility, and with that responsibility comes more confidence. We enjoy being their coaches and giving them input but letting them call the plays. They know they won't have the full picture of their future, but we encourage them to "do the next right thing" and trust that God will lead them to the next step and the next.

Discuss Money

We believe one of the biggest mistakes of parents is not instilling practical perspectives about money in their kids. When they leave home, if they don't have good values and practices about money, they're a train wreck waiting to happen. Financial expert Dave Ramsey gives a lot of good advice to parents of adolescents, including:

- Show your kids how to make a budget. Work with them to list everything they buy, and help them develop a plan. Make sure it's *their* budget, not yours for them. That's the only way they'll be motivated to follow it.
- Teach them the importance of setting long-range savings goals. If they're actually going to save, it's important for you to avoid buying them big-ticket items they really want. You may choose to provide matching funds for a car or something else that's very expensive, but don't make it too easy for them.
- No credit cards! Ramsey says, "Don't fill their brains with that 'you need a card to build your credit' crap. That's for people who want to make a life habit of borrowing money. Break that cycle before it even gets started by teaching them to not borrow."
- Expect the discipline of saving and spending on a budget to make a difference in other aspects of your teenager's life. Discipline,

self-control, and delayed gratification are important traits in health, schoolwork, a career, and marriage.
- Ramsey concludes, "Love your kids enough to properly teach them about being adults. If they are deeply in debt with a marriage hanging by a thread in thirty years, what are you going to say? 'Sorry, son, that I didn't teach you better... but at least you thought I was cool when you were a teen!'"[93]

Another lesson to teach your kids regarding money is the importance of returning the tithe to God through your local church. We don't give *to* the church, we give *through* the church. The word *tithe* in the Bible is defined as one tenth. If we teach our kids by example to give one tenth out of every dollar they make, they'll always know they're living under God's umbrella of protection and provision. The tithe belongs to God, and when we're faithful in honoring God by returning what belongs to Him, God always provides for us, and in fact, He gives us more so we can be even more generous. We get to give, we don't give to get. Commit to making the shift in this area and watch what God will do. It's impossible to out-give God. If you don't believe it, read Malachi 3:10 and let God prove it to you!

> *Generosity is not a single act; It is a way of seeing and thinking.*
> —Brian Houston[94]

Changing Roles

When your kids were very young, you were god-like: big, authoritative, and strong. As they got older and they learned to manage their growing autonomy, parenting became more like coaching. As they leave home, you're a trusted mentor. And later, when they have their careers and

---

93 Dave Ramsey, "How to Teach Teenagers about Money," *Ramsey Solutions*, https://www.daveramsey.com/blog/teach-teenagers-about-money.

94 Brian Houston, *Live, Love, Lead*, 56.

family, you're still their parent, but you become more of a peer. Don't be afraid of this transition. Embrace it—for their sake and yours.

TRUST GOD

We're not on our own as we help our kids grow and thrive as young adults. We can trust God to guide us as much as we trust him to guide them. We trust him to lead them on the path He wants them to go. Jesus prayed, "Not my will but yours be done." That's our prayer for our kids: "Lord, I want what you want for them more than what I want for them . . . because you know far more than I do!" God always leads people into and through times of struggle. Hard times don't necessarily mean our children are missing God's will. They may be right in the middle of it. We trust that He will teach them lessons they can only learn from trusting Him in good times and bad.

We trust God to use failure in their lives. We're not talking about accidents or other things that are out of their control. These are their personal mistakes. We have them, and they have them. When they happen, we trust they'll learn to be completely honest with God and honest with at least one other person—but maybe not us. And we hope God will show them more than ever the depth of His love and forgiveness so repentance brings them joy instead of shame.

We trust God to bless them with enough success and joy that they realize He is a wonderful Father who delights in them. And we trust God to correct them when they're getting off track. We trust God to bring people into their lives to encourage them and challenge them to be all they can be.

We've looked at five important shifts in this book. This last one, modeling a life of faith and integrity, will shape the lives of our children while they're with us and for the rest of their lives. In John's last short letter, he put parenting in perspective: "I could have no greater joy than to hear that my children are following the truth" (3 John 4, NLT).

Have you made the shift? If not, it's time.

THINK ABOUT IT:
1) The goal of parenting is to give our children what they need to be healthy, independent, creative, loving adults. Do you agree or disagree with that statement? How do some parents get it wrong? What are some of the results?
2) Describe the ways your parents gave you roots and wings. How could they have done it better?
3) What is your vision for your children? Why does having one matter?
4) What impact do we have on our kids when we communicate, "I love you," "I'm proud of you," and "You're really good at..."
5) What are some ways you can help your children have a healthy concept of money?
6) Does the idea of changing roles in parenting make sense to you? Why or why not?
7) What is your level of anxiety or confidence that your kids will become strong, responsible, loving adults? Explain your answer.

DO IT:
Answer and discuss these questions as a family:
1) Identify which of the five shifts in this book is most important to you.
2) What difference will it make when you implement it?
3) Define your three next steps to apply the principles in this book.

NOTES

APPENDIX

FAMILY SHIFT PERSONALITY TEST

THE AVATAR PERSONALITY ASSESSMENT

This assessment helps you discover your dominant personality type and how it shapes your natural tendencies in thinking, feeling, and acting. Follow the steps below to complete the test and interpret your results.

Instructions

1) Read Each Statement: For each personality category, review the descriptive statements carefully.
2) Select Your Response: Circle or mark one of the options: ALWAYS, SOMETIMES, or NEVER.
   - ALWAYS: This describes you consistently.
   - SOMETIMES: This describes you occasionally.
   - NEVER: This rarely or never describes you.
3) Score Each Category: Assign points to your responses:
   - ALWAYS = 2 points
   - SOMETIMES = 1 point
   - NEVER = 0 points

4) **Calculate Your Total:** Add the points for each category to identify your dominant personality type.

Scoring and Interpretation
1) **Determine Your Highest Score:** The category with the highest total points is your dominant personality type.
2) **Tied Scores:** If you have tied scores in two or more categories, you may have a blend of those personalities. Ask a family member or close friend to share from their perspective what characteristic they see displayed the most to confirm which avatar is most dominant.

Personality Descriptions
1) **Ninja**
   Traits: Methodical, detail-oriented, thorough, and prefers working behind the scenes.
   Influence: Ninjas excel in tasks requiring precision and are driven by the satisfaction of completing projects efficiently. Their focus on details influences their analytical thinking and dependable nature.
   Potential Weaknesses: Ninjas can get bogged down in details, leading to perfectionism or procrastination. They may struggle with delegation or feel overlooked when their contributions are behind the scenes.
2) **Mastermind**
   Traits: Visionary, team-builder, inspirational, and goal-oriented.
   Influence: Masterminds excel in leadership roles by inspiring others. Their big-picture thinking drives their passion for collaboration and achievement.
   Potential Weaknesses: Masterminds may overlook details in favor of the big picture, causing missteps in execution. Their strong vision can sometimes lead to stubbornness or difficulty accepting feedback.

3) **Trailblazer**
   Traits: Independent, resourceful, innovative, and determined.
   Influence: Trailblazers are natural problem-solvers, always looking for better ways to achieve goals. They thrive on challenges, fueling their creative and forward-thinking mindset.
   Potential Weaknesses: Trailblazers may become impatient with others who don't match their pace or vision. Their independence can lead to reluctance in asking for help or collaboration.
4) **Guardian**
   Traits: Compassionate, protective, nurturing, and service-oriented.
   Influence: Guardians are driven by empathy and a strong desire to protect and support others. Their caring nature influences their decisions and relationships.
   Potential Weaknesses:: Guardians may overextend themselves or struggle to set boundaries, leading to burnout. Their protective instincts can sometimes come across as controlling or overbearing.
5) **Social Genius**
   Traits: Outgoing, friendly, networking-savvy, and approachable.
   Influence: Social Geniuses excel in building relationships and creating harmony. Their charisma drives their ability to connect with and influence people effectively.
   Potential Weaknesses: Social Geniuses may struggle with consistency or follow-through, as they are easily distracted by new people or opportunities. Their need for approval can sometimes lead to superficial relationships.

The Personality and Passions assessments help you see how your God-given wiring shapes the way you interact with others, solve problems, and approach everyday life.

WHICH AVATAR ARE YOU?

Ninja—People may never see the NINJA, but they know you were there by the trail of completion left behind you!			
I am task-oriented.	ALWAYS	SOMETIMES	NEVER
I love details.	ALWAYS	SOMETIMES	NEVER
I am very thorough.	ALWAYS	SOMETIMES	NEVER
I would rather be behind the scenes than in the crowd.	ALWAYS	SOMETIMES	NEVER

Mastermind—If you see a great team, you can bet there is a MASTERMIND behind it!			
I am a team builder.	ALWAYS	SOMETIMES	NEVER
I consider myself very motivational/ inspirational.	ALWAYS	SOMETIMES	NEVER
I can rally people behind the vision.	ALWAYS	SOMETIMES	NEVER
I love when people come together to accomplish a goal.	ALWAYS	SOMETIMES	NEVER

Appendix **239**

Trailblazer—The trailblazer loves a challenge and will rise to it without fail every time!			
I am very independent.	ALWAYS	SOMETIMES	NEVER
I show ownership and initiative.	ALWAYS	SOMETIMES	NEVER
I love to figure out how to do things better.	ALWAYS	SOMETIMES	NEVER
I can tackle just about anything.	ALWAYS	SOMETIMES	NEVER

Guardian—The guardian is no wimp, though; just try to hurt those close to a GUARDIAN, and you'll get your behind kicked!			
I am compassionate.	ALWAYS	SOMETIMES	NEVER
I am a protector.	ALWAYS	SOMETIMES	NEVER
I am a cultivator.	ALWAYS	SOMETIMES	NEVER
I love meeting needs of those around me.	ALWAYS	SOMETIMES	NEVER

Social Genius—Every time with the social genius is like the first time!			
I am very outgoing.	ALWAYS	SOMETIMES	NEVER
I am very friendly.	ALWAYS	SOMETIMES	NEVER
I am a networker.	ALWAYS	SOMETIMES	NEVER
I naturally make people feel at ease around me.	ALWAYS	SOMETIMES	NEVER

Copyright 2025. All rights reserved by ReThink Life Church. www.rethinklife.com

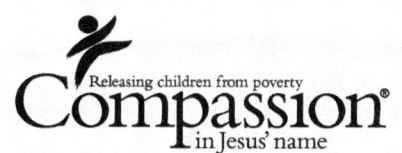

Lissa, Dorcas and Nance
TANZANIA

Helping Kids, Helping Families

Ground your family in purpose and strengthen your faith in Christ by helping release a child from poverty in Jesus' name.

Sponsor a child today!

Compassion.com/twf

Compassion Explorer is our quarterly magazine built to inspire kids to advocate for children living in poverty.

Check it out today!
Explorer.Compassion.com

WINNING RESOURCES FOR YOUR FAMILY

The Winning Family is your go-to source for practical wisdom, faith-based inspiration, and real-life tools to help you raise strong kids, build a thriving marriage, and create a home that wins.

SCAN HERE to help you (win) where it matters most — <u>at home</u>!

thewinningfamily.com

TAKE THE GUESSWORK OUT OF PARENTING &
START ⟨WINNING⟩ AT HOME

Every parent needs a mentor. This one-of-a-kind, **12-week** mentorship gives you the clarity, confidence, and proven plan you need to build a family that wins at home.

What Is The Winning Family Mentorship?

Led by Rodney & Michelle Gage—pastors, parents, and founders of The Winning Family—this mentorship combines biblical wisdom, research-backed tools, and step-by-step guidance to strengthen your marriage, deepen your faith, and raise resilient kids who love Jesus.

SCAN HERE
FOR MORE DETAILS

thewinningfamily.com

www.ingramcontent.com/pod-product-compliance
Lightning Source LLC
LaVergne TN
LVHW020439271125
826467LV00005B/24